Welcome to
Pop-Up Studio!

Publishing Details

Printed in Canada
ISBN 978-1-9991717-2-8 (softcover)

Published by Circularity Press
© 2021 Misty Paterson and Janice Novakowski. All rights reserved.
www.popupstudioed.com

Edited by Jessica Sherer
Proofread by Alison Strobel
Design by Danielle Connor | 2nd Edition design updated by Jazmin Welch
Photos by Alyssa Dawson Photography: *pp. 1, 5, 7 (all but top right), 8, 12, 18, 24, 25, 27, 29, 30, 32, 42, 50, 53, 54, 56, 69 (bottom), 79, 88, 100, 104 (left),108, 109, 110, 111, 113, 115, 117, 119, 120, 122 (top), 124, 131 (bottom left), 132 (left), 141, 143, 147, 151.*
Photos taken at Nido de Montessori: *pp. 59, 69 (top right), 74, 86, 91, 122 (bottom), 140.*
Sandra Vander Schaaf Photography: *pp. 16, 65, 78, 104 (right).*
Unsplash: *pp. 14, Mel Poole; 55, Taylor Wilcox; 67, Soundtrap.*

Planning templates from this book are designed to be used by individual educators. These can be customized and reproduced for educational/training purposes (up to 100 copies per page, per year). The following must appear on customized publications: Reproduced from *Pop-Up Studio* by Misty Paterson with Janice Novakowski.

Media, speaking, and sales inquiries: info@popupstudioed.com

You create positive change when you buy this book. We donate a portion of your purchase to charities that provide children access to direct experiences that build a sense of hope, discovery, and possibility. Thank you!

2nd EDITION

POP-UP Studio

RESPONSIVE TEACHING FOR TODAY'S LEARNERS

A DESIGN GUIDE FOR PLAYFULLY IGNITING AGENCY, ARTISTRY, AND UNDERSTANDING WITH CONCEPTS AND MATERIALS ANYWHERE

MISTY PATERSON

WITH JANICE NOVAKOWSKI

Foreword by H. Lynn Erickson, Ed.D.

Dedication

To the children, families, and educators who inspire us. Your insights, questions, and hopes kindle our learning journey.

Acknowledgements

Firstly, we extend our deepest gratitude to our families, friends, and colleagues: you are our biggest inspiration, our champions and cheerleaders. This project would not have been realized without you.

We stand on the shoulders of educational giants whose work grounds the structure, framework, and examples held within these pages. We have curated ideas that enrich our lives as educators and parents. Specifically, we want to spotlight the following curriculum theorists, professors, and researchers. Their theoretical contributions are in bold.

Hannah Arendt
and David Smith

Anew

David Jardine

Abundance and Authenticity

Anne Phelan

The 4As Guiding Principles

· · · · · · · · · · · · · · · · · · · ·

Ron Ritchhart
and Project Zero

Routine and Agency

H. Lynn Erickson,
Lois Lanning, and
Rachel French

Concept- Based

Ann Pelo

Studio

· · · · · · · · · · · · · · · · · · · ·

Veronica Pacini-Ketchabaw,
Sylvia Kind, and
Laurie L. M. Kocher

Role of Materials and Documentation/ Narration

· · · · · · · · · · · · · · · · · · · ·

Karen Meyer

Awareness

John Dewey

Aesthetics and Experience

We also want to thank the teacher-researchers at Opal School, Dr. Lorna Earl, Dr. Helen Timperley, and countless other caring and wise thinkers for offering living examples of thoughtful inquiry to educators around the world. Your leadership, wisdom, and passion ignites our work!

To learn more about the above ideas, please take up the References and Recommended Readings lists at the back of the book. Further resources can be found at *www.popupstudioed.com.*

We offer Pop-Up Studio in service to the children and educators we respectfully call our "thinking partners."

Foreword by H. Lynn Erickson, Ed.D.

Pop-Up Studio: Responsive Teaching for Today's Learners, by Misty Paterson with Janice Novakowski, achieves that delicate balance between creativity and intellectual rigour. Readers are invited into Pop-Up Studio through the intentional juxtaposition of colourful design elements, engaging language, and interactive elements to honour the reader, nudge thinking, and inspire agency.

What a pleasure it has been to see how Misty took her intensive training on Concept-Based Curriculum and Instruction from the Lynn Erickson and Lois Lanning Certification Institute and combined it with her prior knowledge and experience to create *Pop-Up Studio*—this beautiful design guide to help educators pop up learning to a three-dimensional experience that is rigorous, personal, and purposeful. Pop-Up Studio develops the notion of "craft" as artistry in teaching and learning. Craft in Pop-Studio attends to such elements as intention, mindfulness, pride, elegance, novelty, and innovation.

This book is creative—from the title "Pop-Up Studio" through the pages filled with creative suggestions for helping students interact with materials and manipulatives to more deeply understand transferrable concepts and ideas. This book is intellectual—that is, it both requires and develops intellect. The Concept-Material-Experience (CME) Design Framework clearly illustrates how to create the synergy between lower- and higher-order thinking. Pop-Up Studio is steeped in thoughtful pedagogy that develops the intellect and exemplifies the latest brain and learning research related to building conceptual understanding, engaging and motivating learners, and creating personal relevance. A major goal of the CME Design Framework is conceptual understanding.

Pop-Up Studio: Responsive Teaching for Today's Learners is logically arranged and takes the reader effortlessly through the CME Design Framework providing a gallery of suggestions and classroom vignettes. The book is a treasure trove of tools. The tools provoke your thinking, engage your visual interest, and assist in planning Pop-Up Studio experiences while remaining accessible and playful. This beautifully crafted design guide helps educators create learning engagements that develop student agency by inviting personal interest.

The 4As (Abundance, Authenticity, Awareness, and Anew) provide assessment lenses and a reflective cycle for the teacher and students. The purpose of The 4As are to bring us closer to the learner and to their experience of learning. Each "A" nudges us forward in practical ways to deepen learning and open up new possibilities and pathways.

Teaching and learning should be joyful. This book is joyful yet practical. The authors successfully accomplished a difficult balance: supporting the need for a pedagogical design structure that meets standards and expectations, while still engaging both teachers and students as critical and creative thinkers.

> Pop-Up Studio reminds us how important it is to focus on the student as learner, and to draw out creativity as well as the intellect in both the student and the teacher. I love this book!
>
> —H. Lynn Erickson, Ed.D.

Pop-Up Studio Defined

Pop-Up Studio is a process and platform for creating hands-on experiences to help learners playfully generate and transfer ideas with agency, artistry, and understanding.

Pop-Up, because the taught curriculum becomes a sensorial experience that supports conceptual understanding. Learners draw upon concepts and hands-on materials to seek deeper meaning, beauty, and significance within and across disciplines, at school, at home, in the community, or anywhere!

Studio, because we aim to create a studio-like environment for learners to think and create like studio artists who envision, experiment, and express creatively whether in the science lab, the kitchen, the gym, or the generalist's classroom (Hetland et al., 2013).

Playfully, because we prioritize and nurture choice, wonder, and delight in everything we do (Mardell et al., 2016).

Agency, because we want learners to embody the capacity and propensity to initiate positive action in any situation (Ferguson et al., 2015).

Artistry, because we are creatives and we value craft. We want learners to develop craft within every subject area we teach, such as writer's craft, speaker's craft, etc. We believe that craft is found in any discipline where humans design something skillfully and creatively (Eisner, 2002).

Understanding, because we want learners to see patterns and relationships within and across the subject areas. We want to teach content, concepts, and competencies so students understand why, where, when, and how to apply their learning in new contexts (Erickson et al., 2017).

Table of Contents

Pop-Up Studio Philosophy

"

The aim of education ought to be conceived of as
the preparation of artists...individuals who have
developed the ideas, the sensibilities, the skills, and the
imagination to create work that is well proportioned,
skillfully executed, and imaginative, regardless of the
domain in which an individual works.

The highest accolade we can confer upon someone
is to say that he or she is an artist whether as a
carpenter or a surgeon, a cook or an engineer,
a physicist or a teacher.

What I think many of us want is not only a form
of educational practice whose features, so to speak,
'design us,' but a form of educational practice that
enables students to learn how to design themselves.

Thus, it might be said that at its best, education
is a process of learning how to become the architect
of our own education. It is a process that does not
terminate until we do.

"

ELLIOT EISNER

Welcome!

If you are teaching young people in the 21st century, you know we are at a new juncture: We are shaping the most materially endowed, the most digitally connected, most culturally diverse, and the most knowledge-rich generation to date—at a time when all of us are the most physically disconnected (McCrindle, 2020). As educators, we know that our positive influence resides in our *response*-ability: the way we take up young people's questions, ideas, and dreams.

This book is for fellow teachers, administrators, curriculum consultants, professional development designers, homeschool parents, or anyone who wants to kindle caring connections with today's learners by meaning-making together. The following pages aim to show you how we are *already* positioned as creatives to construct new definitions of school, work, and even well-being. Now is the time to bring Eisner's (2002) vision for agency and artistry to teaching using the Pop-Up Studio platform.

Briefly stated, Pop-Up Studio is an empowering approach for building responsible relationships to the materials in our lives, to the ideas we've inherited, and, ultimately, to each other and the natural world. Pop-Up Studio began as a phrase to capture the thoughtful interplay that emerges when teachers, learners, materials, and concepts converge in intentional and transformative ways. It was birthed out of a desire to articulate creative processes and opportunities that:

- Feel natural to learning,
- Align with the rights of children (such as the right to play, access to the arts, and an education to help them serve the world),
- Reflect current neuroscience, and
- Frame the teacher's role as a pedagogical artist.

> *What educational possibilities awaken when we see ourselves as artists of our craft?*

WHAT IS A PEDAGOGICAL ARTIST?

Pedagogue:
A teacher or schoolmaster (*Merriam-Webster*, n.d.)

Artist:
A human who makes change happen by doing generous work that might not work (Godin, 2020).

If teaching is art, then we are *all* artists who renovate ideas and make change happen. You can see that I'm not referring to painting, drawing, sculpting, dance, music, or any other fine or performing art, but rather a broader concept of artist. Being an artist speaks to, "the combination of talent, skill, craft, and point of view that brings new light to old problems" (Godin, 2020, p. 3). Being a pedagogical artist, then, acknowledges that teaching is a generous, creative process that, when successful, transforms someone.

BECOMING AN ARTIST: MISTY'S JOURNEY

While I have been a pedagogue for over 20 years, I did not always see myself as an "artist." I trained as a generalist classroom teacher. I viewed artists as exceptional individuals who used their inherited and refined creativity to express ideas and convey emotion with ease and perfection. After all, every encounter I had with the arts was with a finished, polished product. I recall viewing visual and performing art with the same thought: "I wish I could do that. I wish I had the talent." I didn't see any connections between being an artist and being a teacher.

The dichotomy of artist/non-artist became a barricade that separated me from other creatives. I was in an uncertain state of, "When I'm good enough, I'll make this or try that. When I've rehearsed enough, I'll put myself out there." This thinking trap robbed me of joy and starved me of the thing I needed most to thrive: connection.

Fortunately, ongoing conversations with Reggio Emilia researchers, Studio Thinking authors from Project Zero at Harvard University, countless master teachers like my contributing author, Janice Novakowski, and hundreds of inspiring students, taught me that art is not (always) about creating a polished product using one's innate talents. On the contrary, artistic ways of knowing and living are essential to being human.

Conversations with creative thinkers renovated my concept of art and artist. But I know not every teacher has had these same transformative opportunities. I want to change that.

It took me two degrees, numerous workshops, and ongoing mentorships to realize and now declare: I am an artist! I embody an artistic sensibility and enact studio thinking as my way of being in the world as a pedagogical consultant and classroom teacher. I feel free to bring my appreciation for beauty, creativity in solving challenges, and love of crafting multimodal learning invitations to bear on my practice. I'm experiencing a joy in my career that I wish everyone could experience. That's why I wrote the book you have in your hands.

WHAT IS THE VALUE IN SEEING MYSELF AS A PEDAGOGICAL ARTIST?

You deserve joy in teaching and learning, and now, it's at your fingertips. I believe we are better when we collectively support one another to cultivate connected, creative learning communities, so let's pursue artistic, joyful teaching together.

If "every education system is only as good as the teachers who provide the hands-on schooling," (UNESCO Institute for Statistics, 2016, p. 1), imagine the pedagogical implications if we all stepped into our artistry! I support you to see yourself as a pedagogical artist and every teaching decision as an artistic choice.

Throughout our combined 50-plus years as teachers and researchers, Janice and I have navigated the complex roles school stakeholders play in diverse education settings. We've found ourselves between the call of responding to student needs in the moment and the burdening demands of leading a classroom or school with competing mandates.

We have struggled in situations where, as professor and author John Spencer (2017) claims:
> ...schools talk about innovation but they fail to trust their teachers to innovate in their own practice. Leaders pass out sets of boxed curriculum and we end up with master chefs who are stuck making Hamburger Helper or master artists doing paint by numbers.

If this resonates with you, please know: We get it. We see you. We want to help.

Years of balancing learner engagement with competing directives has taught us this: responsiveness comes alive when we are tuned into our students and we lean into our artistry. We believe you are a master artist and your students are collaborators in the learning journey. In the pages ahead, you'll find ideas to inspire creative meaning-making and kindle connection with your learners. Let's get started, shall we?

You deserve joy in teaching and learning, and now, it's at your fingertips. I believe we are better when we collectively support one another to cultivate connected, creative learning communities, so let's pursue artistic, joyful teaching together.

HOW DO I CULTIVATE A RESPONSIVE LEARNING ENVIRONMENT FOR TODAY'S LEARNERS?

Before we can start building a learning space, we have to better understand today's learners and their unique needs. Kids born between 2010 and 2024, known as Generation Alpha, are "the most materially endowed generation ever, the most technologically savvy generation ever, and they will enjoy a longer lifespan than any previous generation" (McCrindle, 2020). And while researchers like Dan Woodman, a sociology professor at the University of Melbourne, caution against forcing the wide range of human experience into generational labels and characteristics (Pinsker, 2020), young people today are certainly growing up in a world quite different from that of their parents and teachers.

With the basic profile of Gen Alpha in mind, let's return to the question of cultivating a responsive learning atmosphere for today's learners, and let's start with examining our own learning process.

What do you do when you want to learn something? If you're like me and many of the students I teach, you reach for a piece of technology. When I ask my own children, "Where did you learn how to do that?" 90 percent of the time, they say, "YouTube." Is this true for you as well?

If you have access to technology and the internet, then you likely swim in the pool of learning possibilities, too. From free courses and tutorials to social media and online teaching resources, we are living in information-rich times where entry into "how to" do something can be fast, easy, and cheap. Customized learning options and communication tools are at the ready. As Unicef (n.d.-a) notes, cultivating a responsive learning environment through access to quality materials for educational purposes is crucial for all learners in the digital age.

Still, while the world is at our fingertips digitally, we are more physically distanced from each other and increasingly starved for human connection (Carrington, 2019). Herein lies a tension that we can reframe as an opportunity to tap into our creativity and reconnect face-to-face (in person or digitally) with this generation. We can listen and learn from our students to find out what they crave and need from us as educators.

When I confer with young people, the general consensus is that they want formal learning to be hands-on, but they also desire harder work. What does that mean? My students say they want learning to be "beyond marks" (Paterson, 2010), meaning they want "school" to be a place where they are seen as capable of taking on challenges that have a tangible impact. Even my youngest learners ask, "Can I take this home to show my loved ones?"

Generally, teachers have the challenge (and opportunity) to integrate everyday materials in a way that invites learners to be thinkers and producers, not just consumers, within their educational activities. We want to guide them in investigating and interrogating their learning rather than simply completing tasks.

As pedagogical artists, we'll start by fostering critical, creative, and conceptual thinking by asking questions that frame the subject matter (let's say, the human body) through a bigger picture concept (like systems). Playing to authentic experiences, we'll contextualize and internalize the content at hand, all while getting messy with materials, just like experts do. Then, we'll act on our learning with a new and broader audience.

This is not just learning that transfers, it's learning that leads. Remember, as Eisner (2002) said, the goal is "a form of educational practice that enables students to learn how to design themselves" (p. 14) instead of being designed by someone or something else.

More specifically, this book is filled with ideas to help you answer those questions in your specific context. The pages ahead are designed to support you in co-creating responsive educational experiences with learners using planning and assessing competencies to empathize, envision, design, experiment, improvise, and pivot as learning unfolds. This is what Pop-Up Studio is all about.

If you're craving more connection and creativity with your students, and you feel you have some autonomy in your teaching, you are in the right place! Please join us in attuning to our students and their learning processes in the name of amplifying agency, artistry, and understanding wherever we are!

Support Learning with Artistry

So what does it mean to support learning as a pedagogical artist within the Pop-Up Studio context?

Let's unpack the question and put it into context by introducing you to some friends and colleagues who, like Janice and I, work feet-on-the-ground with students in real time. We hope you find resonance with their stories and inspiration within our responses.

DOES IT MEAN TEACHING TOWARDS UNDERSTANDING? *Yes!*

Meet our friend, Kris. This is what they are exploring:

"I've recently attended professional development workshops that stress the importance of learners constructing understanding (of the deeper concepts within the respective study/discipline) in addition to content and skill mastery. I've learned that, as an educator, I can't simply transmit understanding to learners, regardless of age. Instead, I can work towards creating conducive conditions to help learners make sense of subject-worthy questions and puzzles. Learners 'sort out' their findings by constructing transferrable understandings. These understandings, or Big Ideas, are based on ideas/concepts that hold true across time, place, and situation."

You might be wondering:

What does it mean to focus teaching towards understanding, beyond fact and skill acquisition alone? What do we consider as we seek to create conducive conditions for transferrable learning? The CME Design Framework and the POWR Coaching Cycle take up these challenges with a special focus on the role of play and materials. Please explore the resources in the References and Recommended Readings to gain further clarity into these timely paradigm shifts.

DOES IT MEAN DESIGNING FOR PLAYFUL LEARNING WITHIN CONSTRAINTS? Yes!

Meet our friend, Jocelyn. This is what they are experiencing:

"I see how calm, relaxed, and engaged my students (and my own children) are when they're playing. As a professional, I also prefer learning when I can make choices, and when the process feels more fluid, collaborative, and honouring. I'm reading about the value of play in learning—not only in Early Years contexts but throughout the grades as the content load usually increases. Play takes time and is usually self-initiated. My school day is highly scheduled and adult-initiated. I am also working alone in a bit of a silo at times, which doesn't feel very playful."

Do you crave ideas to design playful learning opportunities when time, instructional, environmental, and budget constraints are real challenges?

This book shares images, lists, and prompts from collaborative efforts with learners and educators. May these become starting points to tap into your inner curator and your community resources.

DOES IT MEAN POPPING UP MY REGULAR PENCIL-AND-PAPER ACTIVITIES TO A SENSORIAL EXPERIENCE WHERE TINKERING WITH IDEAS AND HANDS-ON MATERIALS ARE CONNECTED TO LEARNING GOALS? Yes!

Meet our friend, Brin. This is what they are noticing:

"The learners I work with are most engaged when learning is hands-on and experiential. During these times, many learners seem focused on the learning journey itself. As an educator, I also feel more engaged in the learning process and connected to the learners themselves. I love Pinterest, STEAM-inspired kits, and other DIY activities, but I'm not always sure how to connect these to my curricular goals."

Let's adapt these inspiration sources so they facilitate deeper understanding.

Inspired by Concept-Based Curriculum and Instruction (CBCI), the CME Design Framework illustrates how concepts can frame learning experiences to forge new thinking pathways.

Are you curious about supporting learners in designing their own playful learning experiences while gaining conceptual understanding? Me too!

The Concept-Material-Experience (CME) Design Framework is designed to be accessible and flexible enough for students to create their own Pop-Up Studios!

Pop-Up Studio Background

> "
> Teachings come from everywhere
> when you open yourself to them.
> That's the trick of it, really,
> open yourself to everything and
> everything opens itself to you.
> "

RICHARD WAGAMESE

The History of Pop-Up Studio

HOW DID THIS BOOK COME TO BE?

It all started in 2016 when my home province mandated a concept-based, competency-driven curriculum model. Changing pedagogical models created a massive shift for many educators I worked with. Since I had established myself as a concept-based teacher and advocate, I became a go-to resource for schools within the province, hosting hands-on, how-to workshops—"pop-up classrooms," as I called them—on professional development days.

Those teacher-to-teacher opportunities grew into more complex projects and long-term contracts aimed at helping teachers, administrators, and parents rethink how we teach to better honour how our students learn. Because of the studio-like aesthetic and focus on critical, creative, and conceptual thinking, the "pop-up" workshops became fondly known as "pop-up studios."

Sense-making journeys are often tangled treasure troves, and mine is no different. In 2014, I met Janice Novakowski, a district teacher consultant who shared similar interests and passions. Janice introduced me to her Math Studio, first by creating a mini studio experience in my classroom and then in her physical classroom-turned-studio.

I was immediately hooked by her interpretation of our provincial curriculum and complementary Reggio-inspired practices. Learning in the studio felt natural: imaginative, focused, joyful. Janice is the original inspiration behind my concept of studio teaching. Pop-Up Studio wouldn't exist without her!

By 2017, teacher friends, like Kris, Jocelyn, and Brin, asked me to record my "elegantly simple" (per Kath Murdoch's endorsement) approach to planning "popped-up" learning experiences with concepts and materials. I recall stating, "But there are already so many great books. What can I offer?"

Once again, Janice came alongside me. With her support, I mustered the courage and clarity to put pen to paper, and we crafted the first iteration of *Pop-Up Studio: Playfully Igniting Agency, Artistry, and Understanding with Concepts and Compelling Materials.* Thank you, Janice!

With two degrees in curriculum and instruction, over 20 years of experience, and a track record of turning schools around, it's safe to say that Pop-Up Studio is more than my career; it's my passion. Today, I think of myself as a curriculum and pedagogy artist and the classroom as a canvas. I created this book for you with love, and with it, I hope to inspire artistry in your classroom or school.

Now, let's pop it up!

I wrote *Pop-Up Studio* as the answer to a recurring question: How do we bring learning to life in our classrooms? The answer isn't another worksheet or app—it's *you.* Pop-Up Studio offers an empowering approach to bring the curiosity and ingenuity we want to foster in our classrooms.

The Pop-Up Studio Process

WHAT CAN THIS BOOK DO FOR ME?

Put simply, this book is a guide to bring curriculum to life by being a pedagogical artist and learning activist. A learning activist is committed to "inquire with students into student understandings and misconceptions and to draw flexibly on a range of strategies to promote a particular student's learning at that particular time" (Le Fevre et al., 2016, p. 312).

I fully recognize that there is no one way or *right* way to activate and sustain student engagement. However, I am adding to the collection of voices that centre learning, value the craft of teaching, and amplify student agency. I hope this book continues a dialogue that interrogates industrial models of education in favour of co-creating more learning-driven pedagogies.

Engaged students and an inspired classroom are at your fingertips—literally. Pop-Up Studio integrates a playful, concept-based approach to inquiry to ignite agency, artistry, and understanding with students. The Pop-Up Studio process can be layered and leveraged with the teaching approaches you already use to engage your learners. Here's how it works:

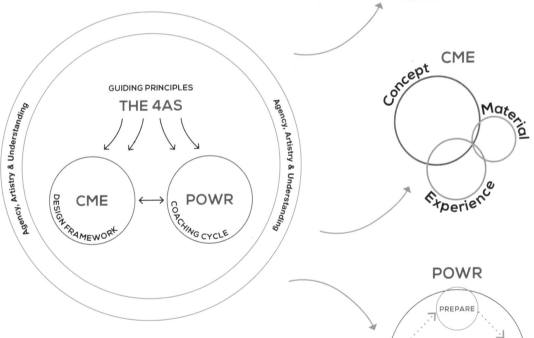

The Pop-Up Studio process aims to develop agency, artistry, and understanding that begin and end with four guiding principles: Abundance, Authenticity, Awareness, and Anew. Educators and learners activate these principles when they design for and enact learning within a Pop-Up Studio experience. The CME Design Framework helps us prepare for learning and the POWR Coaching Cycle aims to ignite and deepen it. As such, the bulk of the book describes these two synergistic frameworks in actionable ways.

THE POP-UP STUDIO GUIDING PRINCIPLES: THE 4AS

We are going for learning that is:

- **Abundant** (rich with multiple perspectives and approaches),
- **Authentic** (real to learners and significant to a broader community),
- **Awareness** building (leading to deeper understanding), and
- **Anew** or novel in some way (concepts are renovated anew for the learner, for the learning group, or for the world at large).

You might notice that the guiding principles all start with the letter "A." We call these principles The 4As.

Abundance

Authenticity

Awareness

Anew

THE POP-UP STUDIO DESIGN FRAMEWORK: CME

CME is a planning framework that makes teaching for understanding playful. Understanding a subject deeply helps us to connect the Big Ideas, or "dots," within our studies and to relate these in coherent, novel, and valuable ways. According to the National Research Council (2000), this is the process of being an expert:

> Deep understanding of subject matter transforms factual information into usable knowledge. A pronounced difference between experts and novices is that experts' command of concepts shapes their understanding of new information: it allows them to see patterns, relationships, or discrepancies that are not apparent to novices. (p. 12)

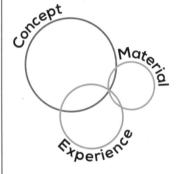

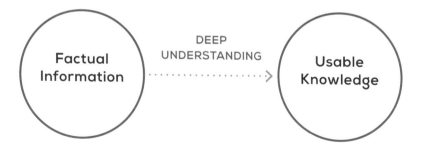

Factual Information ·········> DEEP UNDERSTANDING Usable Knowledge

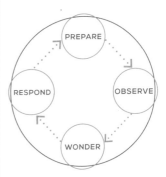

THE POP-UP STUDIO COACHING CYCLE: POWR

POWR is a coaching cycle to spotlight the learning experience and direct it towards the Pop-Up Studio guiding principles (The 4As).

POWR can be a thinking routine to:

1. Refine your CME plans towards The 4As.
2. Confer with learners before, during, and after hands-on learning experiences.

The 4As, CME, and POWR work together to create a dynamic learning cycle when combined with your curiosity and ingenuity. According to the National Academies of Sciences, Engineering, and Medicine (2018), "...humans' drive to understand is powerful. People have an innate capacity to impose meaning on their experiences. This propensity has the potential to be a powerful engine for learning if it is directed at suitable tasks and activities" (p. 151). The aim of The 4As, CME, and POWR—and this whole book, really—is to tap into that innate capacity, helping you grow into a learning activist and pedagogical artist who creates deep connection to the subject areas you teach, to your learners, and to the physical and natural world.

I will introduce The 4As Guiding Principles, CME Design Framework, and POWR Coaching Cycle in context throughout the book to offer real pictures of practice meant to inspire dialogue and possibilities in your setting. Now, let's orient you to the rest of the book!

New Features of *Pop-Up Studio*

HOW CAN I USE THIS BOOK?

Based on reader feedback, I understand that the structure of this book will shape your interpretation of the content. Some readers appreciated the original loose structure, others requested something more descriptive. My hope is to offer a portrait of Pop-Up Studio as an agile and adaptive approach to planning and facilitating playful and purposeful learning experiences with concepts and materials.

This second edition features:

- Additional examples to help you reach a deeper understanding of CME and The 4As as useful tools in your teaching repertoire.
- Some restructuring and rewording of content for enhanced clarity and accessibility.
- New diagrams to simplify the primary intentions of Pop-up Studio, inspiring confidence in your teaching and learning journey.
- More templates and prompts to foster meaningful implementation of your own Pop-Up Studio.

POP-UP STUDIO IS AN ARTFUL APPROACH.

Like other artforms, it embodies a creative zest that doesn't like to be pinned down to a prescriptive structure. My work-around is to draw upon the power of analogy to pull the pieces together in a way that feels cohesive and accessible to you without appearing authoritarian. If needed, feel free to deconstruct your book, take pages apart, and (re)arrange them in your preferred sequence. String the concepts together in a way that feels good for you!

WELCOME TO OUR PRIMARY ANALOGY:
A THREAD-OF-UNDERSTANDING!

Let's imagine reading and using this book like beading a necklace. I'll provide the beads. You bring the thread. Here's how we'll make it work together:

1. Envision each chapter like a box of beads. I'll share beads that have been gifted to me and ones that I've made from scratch. I'll offer "your turn" sections as provocations to form your own ideas and questions (i.e., your own beads).

2. As you read, you'll layer ideas shared in this book with your own knowledge and experience. Just like we want our learners to develop conceptual understanding as they relate ideas together, I want you to craft a connective thread that combines ideas into a dynamic, evergreen continuum. This process can take patience, time, community, and multiple encounters to construct. But you are the perfect person to create this thread! It's the investment in our own cognitive heavy-lifting that results in meaningful, integrated learning.

3. Like past readers, every time you enact the content and revisit your thinking alongside complementary ideas and practices, you'll create new threads that will weave and layer together to form your Pop-Up Studio artistry: a beautiful and personal web that serves you and your learners. We're in this together!

THREAD-OF-
UNDERSTANDING

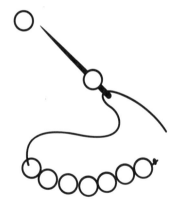

Let's Meet the Beads

HEIRLOOM BEADS:

Think of these beads as the beliefs and practices we bring to our teacher-student relationships. These are our ancestry or inherited beads that help shape our orientation to the learners we serve and to the teaching and learning process. In the next chapter, we ask you to join us in critically reflecting on the dispositions and biases we bring to our practice as part of preparing ourselves for pedagogical interactions.

RESEARCH BEADS:

These beads showcase a sampling of the research findings that anchor Pop-Up Studio within a global network. Consider the research section of the next chapter as a helpful advocate for hands-on learning experiences that guide learners in generating and transferring ideas in meaningful ways.

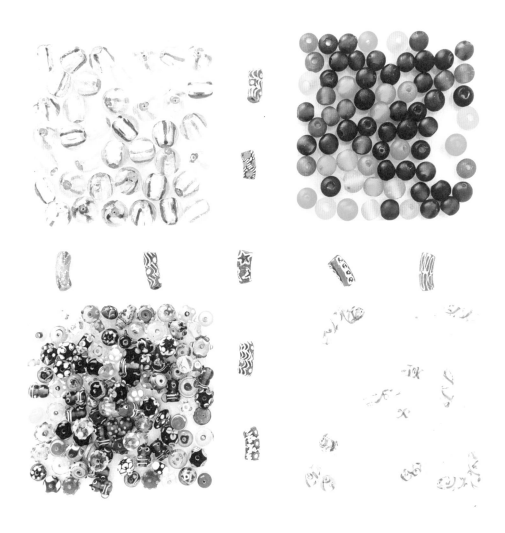

THE 4AS BEADS:

The 4As Guiding Principles become lenses or critical friends to amplify learning experiences when we activate them using the CME Design Framework and the POWR Coaching Cycle. We'll do a quick flyover of Pop-Up Studio in action and then we'll dive deeply into each of The 4As.

A special note about The 4As:

Of all of the chapters in the first iteration of the Pop-Up Studio book, The 4As got the most critique. Dozens of interviews later, I saw why: The 4As don't address assessment of learning. The following paragraphs are intended to bring clarity to the role of The 4A as agents to amplify the learning experience.

I agree with Dr. Lorna Earl (2012) that assessment of learning (or evaluation) continues to be the most privileged form of assessment in classrooms today. It makes sense that you would expect to see rubrics or proficiency scales in the pages ahead. I cannot provide these for you. I hear you ask: But why? Judging how well a learner knows content, understands concepts, and is able to enact required competencies is important!

The book you are holding is not about this kind of assessment. Instead, The 4As are oriented towards two very powerful, transferrable forms of assessment: assessment for learning and assessment as learning. Conversations about learning, and what learners value about their learning, matter, too.

Assessment for learning *helps teachers decide the moves needed next to progress learning. Assessment researcher Dylan Wiliam (2016) likens this process to being a pilot. Throughout the flight, the pilot collects moment-to-moment feedback and makes adjustments as needed.*

Assessment as learning *positions students as protagonists in the assessment experience. Assessment as learning is about students becoming researchers of their own learning, including their sense-making experience and misconceptions. Asking questions like, "How well do I understand what I'm learning?" is part of learning in a Pop-Up Studio. When students are reflective, critical thinkers, they are able to make shifts in their learning and decisions about future directions (Earl, 2012).*

CME BEADS:

These beads comprise the planning framework that makes teaching for understanding playful and improvisational. We will do a deep dive into each of the three key elements—Concept, Material, and Experience—with a case study, examples, and interactive prompts.

POWR BEADS:

These are the key elements in the coaching framework (aka: inquiry cycle or conferring tool) designed to spotlight the learning experience and direct it towards The 4As. You can use POWR to power up learning before, during, and after working alongside students. We'll do a thorough exploration of POWR with vignettes and provocations so you can try it straightaway in your practice.

PREPARATION BEADS:

The template chapter is filled with interactive resources to support you in translating the Pop-Up Studio process for your context. We walk through each phase of the learning experience in a linear sequence. Feel free to use this section as a starting point to guide your initial foray into Pop-Up Studio.

Let's start threading!

Preparing for the Journey:
Beliefs, Practices, and Evidence

> " Grow, it always feels good to grow.
> It feels good to be more wise and more
> aware and go deeper and everything.
> Growth just isn't about growing up.
> Growth is understanding. "

STEVEN, AGE 12

Heirloom Beads: Beliefs and Practices

POP-UP STUDIO ENGAGES US IN A WHOLEHEARTED, INTENTIONAL EXPERIENCE-MAKING PROCESS THAT BEGINS WITH AN EXPANSIVE NOTION OF TEACHING AND LEARNING.

Teaching is a personal and social profession. As leaders of learning, we have tremendous responsibility to set the tone in the spaces and among the people with whom we work. As practising teachers, we know from experience and research that the words we choose, the moves we make, and the resources we use can have dramatic effects on our learners (Bandura, 1993; Gibson & Dembo, 1984, as cited in Schmid, 2018, p. 7). What's more, our beliefs, attitudes, and practices are implicated in how we respond to challenges, and they directly impact our overall well-being (OECD, 2009). Since teacher beliefs and practices directly shape student *and* teacher outcomes, let's take some time to explore them up close.

How might we interrogate our beliefs and practices in playful ways for the betterment of our students and ourselves?

DISCOVERING THE HEIRLOOM BEADS

The heirloom beads serve as a playful analogy and exercise for examining pedagogical beliefs and practices. And I think it's important you know how I discovered them, then abruptly abandoned them, but finally returned to them under the guidance of trusted experts.

Once I decided to use the beaded necklace metaphor, I set to work deciding how best to illustrate related concepts through photography. I immediately thought of a local bead shop and contacted them to see how I might borrow beads for a photoshoot. The store owner was very receptive and invited me to select any materials that may prove helpful.

Fast forward to photoshoot day. I'm looking for beads that best convey the concept of heirloom. I defined heirloom as being passed down, inherited, or holding history. I was directed to African trade beads, some of which were 200 years old. Perfect! We bagged them up and I was on my way.

It wasn't until I held the beads in my hand, hoping to convey the metaphor, while Alyssa was snapping away, that I realized how inappropriate it was for me to use these beads as a non-African. I stopped Alyssa and said, "I can't use these beads this way!"

When I went home and started Googling "African trade beads," I found out that trade beads have been used for centuries to acquire goods and services, and in some cases, those goods were slaves.

I felt that I had an ethical dilemma on my hands: on one hand, these beautiful beads could illustrate the concept of ancestry and tradition, but on the other, they could be triggers that cause pain due to their (potentially) dark history. As a non-African, I want to be sensitive to and deeply respectful of a culture that I am learning from.

I DISTILLED MY QUESTION TO THIS:

Is there a way to showcase the beads that is culturally sensitive and accurately conveys the intended concept of heirloom without evoking potentially harmful associations?

At first, my answer was no. I felt I committed an insensitive act and there was no way to include the beads in this book. I nearly stopped my inquiry. But I didn't. Asking tough questions is uncomfortable but important. In fact, I owe it to you, my readers, to do hard things in the name of growth, empathy, and understanding.

So I wondered: Who could lend some expertise and perspective on trade beads to help me make informed choices? The Museum of Anthropology at the University of British Columbia immediately popped into mind. I met with Dr. Nuno Porto, curator: Africa and South America, a kind and knowledgeable soul. Dr. Porto shared that, based on the information we currently have about the beads, we didn't need to worry that they were used for inappropriate means. He offered sound reasons for showcasing the beads for educational purposes.

My inquiry continued with a discussion regarding cultural appropriation with Silvia Mangue, president of BC Black History Awareness Society, and African artist Jacky Essombe from the African Friendship Society in Vancouver, BC. After explaining my story and ethical dilemma, both Silvia and Jacky gave me their blessing to use the beads and implored me to share this story with you. We all hope that my grappling will inspire discussion in your community about the relationship between ethics, materiality, and inquiry within your pedagogical beliefs and practices. In fact, the exercise below might help you do just that.

Your turn:

Choose a (seemingly) neutral or benign material, like a bead.

ASK: WHERE DOES THIS MATERIAL COME FROM? WHO USES IT? TO WHAT END? WITH WHAT CONSEQUENCES TO OTHERS?

How might our teaching beliefs and practices be interrogated using these same questions? Consider holding a belief or practice up to the light and see what assumptions and possibilities open up for you.

LIVING THE HEIRLOOM BEADS IN THE CLASSROOM

How can we prepare ourselves to create a space where playful inquiry with concepts and materials can thrive?

Based on our experiences with facilitating Pop-Up Studios in various environments, a stance of inquiry, wonder, and curiosity is essential. Janice and I have found the following educator dispositions support this kind of teaching and learning. Please keep in mind that these provocations offer a starting place for conversation. They are not an exhaustive nor an evaluative checklist.

What beliefs and practices might support us to:

Recognize the importance of setting conditions for deep learning?

....

....

....

Appreciate that learning is something that learners do?

....

....

....

Be open-minded?

....

....

....

Be responsive and prepared to scaffold in different ways?

....

....

....

Trust in ourselves and in our learners?

....

....

....

Be clear on our purpose?

....

....

....

Offer intentional choices?

....

....

....

Listen carefully?

....

....

....

Love the learning process?

....

....

....

Take the time to become more knowledgeable about the concepts we teach?

....

....

....

Find joy in creating opportunities?

....

....

....

Be patient with ourselves and our learners?

....

....

....

Take on the role of facilitator as well as director?

....

....

....

Become an ethical curator of ideas, materials, and experiences?

....

....

....

Play to our strengths?

....

....

....

Research Beads: Evidence

DIVERSE VOICES INSPIRE US. WE WANT TO CO-CREATE SPACES WHERE ALL LEARNERS CAN SHARE IDEAS, DEVELOP, AND IMAGINE.

We believe that a democratic environment is foundational to Pop-Up Studio making. Rüsselbæk Hansen and Phelan (2019) argue that democracy is in crisis within and beyond schools. They explain that democracy is not something we can take for granted; rather, it is something that needs to be "re-invented on a daily basis" (p. 2).

Offering spaces where children and teachers have choices within their learning is one way to practise democracy.

> One learns through democracy by doing democracy, and schools can be understood as "playgrounds" for doing so. From this perspective, democracy is not something to be prepared for but something that needs to be aesthetically experienced, lived, and constantly (re)produced. (Rüsselbæk Hansen & Phelan, 2019, p. 2)

Co-creating environments where learners and educators can play with ideas and materials supports democratic learning as we inquire into the world in its current state and reimagine it otherwise (Paterson, 2010).

PLEASE CONSIDER THE FOLLOWING CITATIONS AND STATISTICS AS STARTING PLACES FOR INQUIRY AND AS PROVOCATIVE ARGUMENTS FOR (RE)CREATING AND COMMITTING TO STUDENT-ORIENTED LEARNING ENVIRONMENTS. USE THE SPACES PROVIDED TO RECORD YOUR THOUGHTS.

"The art and science of teaching go beyond the presentation and extraction of information. Artful teachers engage students emotionally, creatively, and intellectually to instill deep and passionate curiosity in learning" (Erickson et al., 2017).

....

....

....

....

....

....

....

"...One's approach to an environment becomes a feature of the environment itself" (Skolnick Weisberg et al., 2014, pp. 277-278).

....

....

....

....

....

....

"Researchers agree that there is no single, well-defined, best way of teaching" (OECD, 2009, p. 97).

....

....

....

....

....

....

....

"Research suggests that feedback is the most effective when it is focused on the task and learning targets; that is, detailed and narrative, not evaluative and graded" (National Academies of Sciences, Engineering, and Medicine, 2018, p. 155).

....

....

....

....

....

....

"Clearly, teachers play an instrumental role in determining whether or not student creativity will be undermined by the use of assessments in the classroom. By being aware of how differing assessment practices can influence student creativity, teachers can make more purposeful efforts to ensure—at least within their own classroom—that the answer to the question 'does assessment kill creativity' is a confident 'No'" (Beghetto, 2005, p. 262).

"...Materials break boundaries [and] open up realms of thought and create new connections" (Odegard, 2012, p. 398).

"The more relevant learning is, the better it is" (OECD/Asia Society, 2018, p. 8).

"...Learning through integrated pedagogies, namely active learning, collaborative and cooperative learning, experiential learning, guided discovery learning, inquiry-based learning, problem-based learning, project-based learning, and Montessori education, can positively affect student learning across social, emotional, physical, creative, and cognitive domains. We find that these pedagogies can altogether create learning experiences for children that are meaningful, actively engaging, iterative, socially interactive, and joyful" (Parker & Thomsen, 2019, p. 7).

99% OF TEACHERS
believe hands-on learning builds students' confidence.

93% OF PARENTS
believe hands-on learning helps children retain knowledge for the future.

89% OF STUDENTS
say hands-on learning helps them learn new things.

LEGO Education (2019)

Your turn:

Find and record below four quotations, statistics, or pieces of evidence that inspire positive action in your context.

....

....

....

....

....

....

....

....

....

....

....

IF YOU WANT TO PUT THIS RESEARCH INTO PRACTICE, WHAT ARE YOUR VERY NEXT STEPS?

1 ....

....

2 ....

....

3 ....

....

Pop-Up Studio in Action: A Flyover

Pop-Up Studio offers a structure that creates purposeful, focused, and playful experiences that use focus concepts and compelling materials to help learners generate and transfer their ideas. The following pages offer a flyover of Pop-Up Studios in action. These vignettes, and those found on pages 92–99, offer examples of how this structure can be used as a single event or as multiple, consecutive experiences that build on each other.

PROFESSIONAL DEVELOPMENT

Professional learning is in full swing in the library. Educators are discussing the concepts of flexibility and responsiveness in teaching. The facilitator springboards their thinking by providing soft wire for each participant to play with and explore, alongside the following guiding questions: How might the wire's attributes help you think about being a responsive educator? What, if any, similarities exist between shaping the wire and shaping your practice? Hands are busy flexing, bending, moulding, and twisting as they transform the wire. A dialogue begins about the significance and challenge of being a flexible educator. The facilitator then offers an article on cultural forces at play in schools (Ritchhart, 2015). With new ideas from the article, the group discusses ways they can be more flexible and responsive with their students, families, and community.

What ideas are sparking for you?

EARLY YEARS

After exploring how two local artists use symbols to communicate beliefs and values, early primary children carefully arrange loose parts on black felt mats. Each child creates a symbol to share important beliefs and values in their family. The children then juxtapose their artwork with their shoulder partner's to look for common conceptual themes and novel ideas.

MIDDLE PRIMARY

Middle primary children work alongside their teacher and a visiting photographer to explore significant places at school. They wonder, "What makes a place significant to a person or people?" Children select a place within their school or school grounds that evokes feeling. Using iPad devices and some simple photography techniques (e.g., rule of thirds), the children attempt to capture this feeling in a photograph. With clipboards, paper, and pencils in hand, they jot down 10 words to describe this place, their feelings about it, and what it reminds them of. The teacher then prints the images and poetry. The teacher and artist work together to create a photo wall, post photos, and list poems in an array. Together with the children, they stand back to look for possible common conceptual themes in response to their question.

EARLY INTERMEDIATE

To launch a unit of study on decimals, fractions, and percentages, early intermediate teachers set up a studio experience with exploratory stations. Each experience invites learners to investigate part/whole relationships. Stations include: measuring while baking (e.g., doubling/halving a recipe), calculating discounts while grocery shopping, creating artwork with pattern blocks, juxtaposing Cuisenaire rods, and ordering fraction cards on an open number line. Learners revisit these stations over a period of three weeks as they problem-pose, problem-solve, and build conceptual understanding together.

What preparations might be needed to pop up in your context?

MIDDLE SCHOOL

Middle school learners have been studying authentic leadership in various contexts. To invite their parents into interactive, playful, and arts-based idea building at the upcoming student-led conferences, learners brainstorm ways to use colourful art media, such as watercolour paints, to relate authentic leadership and colour theory. They pose the questions: What colour(s) best represent authentic leadership to you and why? Do you need to mix the colours to make a new colour to best represent your understanding? What would you name this new colour and why?

CROSS-FACULTY

Five colleagues join together to design a literacy-based pop-up morning. They brainstorm materials to help children think about and relate story elements such as character, plot, and setting. Synergy sparks as they map out their understanding statements and related questions that apply across texts. An example of a transferrable understanding statement (generalization) may be: Authors develop characters to carry the plot. Each educator ensures these learning goals are developmentally appropriate, providing enough depth and breadth for their diverse learners to engage with these story elements through playful interactions.

What images of Pop-Up Studio are taking shape?

The Pop-Up Studio
Guiding Principles: The 4As

> " I think if you were to understand
> something fully, you have to look at all the
> aspects. You can't just look at one thing,
> like one point of view, you have to inquire.
> It is not like [students] should do it to get
> their mark up; they should do it to help
> themselves, discover themselves. "

TRICIA, AGE 13

The 4As Guiding Principles

What are The 4As?

The 4As are principles, or "lenses," that serve as aids to cherish and challenge inquiry-based curriculum and pedagogy. They are my thinking partners to address questions like: How might we awaken new possibilities when a learner seems stuck or disengaged? How might we nudge thinking to new depths? How might we help students become assessors of their own learning experiences?

Assessment questions keep us up at night. Guesswork is stresswork. But if learning is something that learners do, then teachers need tools and competencies to tap into how students interpret their learning experience. The 4As are such a tool for me. I'd like to introduce them to you with the story of how they came to be.

Dr. Anne Phelan, professor at the University of British Columbia, paved the way for me to think about criteria beyond a marking checklist to evaluate an assignment. Dr. Phelan was my Master of Arts supervisor. She was also instrumental in my role as an Adjunct Teaching Professor and Faculty Advisor in an inquiry-based cohort. Through our inquiry seminars, I learned that an academic inquiry aims to be three qualities:

1. *Generous* (multiple perspectives),
2. *Generational* (studied over time), and
3. *Generative* (leading to new learning).

In other words, I discovered how criteria could become principles or indicators of quality inquiry.

To ease my cognitive load, I simplified these aims to three "Gs." I then adopted these "Gs" as a key part of my advising approach. For example, during my faculty advising conferences with preservice teachers, I proposed questions like, "How might we broaden the perspective the children are taking to include diverse viewpoints?"

Questions, inspired by the Gs, transformed the debriefing session into an academic inquiry rather than passing a judgement like, "good lesson." I noticed teacher candidates declaring new insights like, "Oh! I didn't even realize we were perpetuating a stereotype!"

Very quickly, the Gs became my "lenses" and guides-on-the-side to consciously deepen learning in meaningful, responsive ways. Bonus: they were also easy to remember!

Over time, I added a "G" for Genuine and officially renamed them "The 4As"! (If you would like to see the comprehensive rubric that further inspired The 4As, check out the Galileo Network Inquiry Rubric at: *www.galileo.org/rubric.pdf*.)

THE 4AS

Abundance   Authenticity

Awareness   Anew

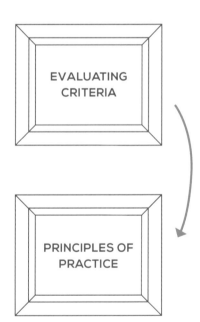

EVALUATING CRITERIA

PRINCIPLES OF PRACTICE

Meet The 4As Beads

The 4As are:

Abundance

TEACHING GOAL:
Turn the seemingly trivial into the transformative.

LEARNING GOAL:
There are so many ways to think about this!

The 4As are
aids to cherish
and challenge
curriculum and
pedagogy.

Authenticity

TEACHING GOAL:
Realize relevancy through real-life relationships and applications.

LEARNING GOAL:
This is important to me, and it's important to others working with this, too.

A BIRD'S-EYE VIEW OF THE 4AS

Based on my master's research and findings, I believe that each A is friendly enough that, with time and ongoing support, learners can use them as self-assessment aids to enhance their own understanding. Let's do a flyover of each A in the following pages to address the *what* and *why* of these Pop-Up Studio Guiding Principles. We'll take up *how* The 4As might power up your learning design, observations, and conversations with students in the CME and POWR chapters.

Awareness

TEACHING GOAL:
Activate "Ahas."

LEARNING GOAL:
Aha! Yes! It's like...

Anew

TEACHING GOAL:
Spark new ideas and share what's swirling.

LEARNING GOAL:
I never thought of it in that way before!

Abundance

There are so many ways to think about this!

Abundance evokes the spirit of generosity and respect. We honour and contribute to the multitude of ways we can come to know and respond to the world through our senses.

For example, every space and every material has its own inherent design, its own story. As Cope and Kalantzis (n.d.) explain, we use multiliteracies to impress meaning into spaces and objects but we also reconstruct meaning from them in return. We then leave traces of meaning behind through our choices and our creative applications. I agree with Eisner (2002) that schools need to attend to the cultivation of literacy in its many forms.

Abundance in our learners begins with us as educators. Embracing the notion of an abundant inquiry means that, "whenever you come upon even the seemingly most trivial of things, it can be experienced, or taken up, or read, or treated as a way into the ways of the world" (Jardine et al., 2006, p. 100). For instance, if we are at the supermarket, we might explore the design of the space, the flow of traffic, the beauty of tidy displays, the trade routes taken to procure exotic produce, the dynamics of exchanging money for goods, etc. The lens of Abundance can reshape what may seem mundane or even trivial at first glance into a transformative investigation.

WHY DOES ABUNDANCE MATTER FOR TODAY'S LEARNERS?

Not only are today's learners the most materially endowed, they are the most digitally connected. Today's learners are growing up in the digital age where technology is changing at an exponential rate. Multiliteracy (being literate in multimodalities) is essential to navigate the way we live, work, and play, especially in a continuously volatile marketplace (New London Group, 1996; Cope & Kalantzis, n.d.; McCrindle, 2020). Understanding the design cycle at play between us and the materials that surround us will continue to be important.

Today's learners belong to an increasingly complex global population. As such, young people need to have the social/emotional and cognitive tools to appreciate, respect, and engage with people and systems whose ideologies may conflict with their own. For example, Dr. Rudine Sims Bishop, professor emerita, Ohio State University, coined the phrase "windows, mirrors, and sliding glass doors" as a way to explain the power media have in shaping identity and theory of mind. She says:

> Children need to see themselves reflected [in mirrors]…to look through other worlds to see how they match up or don't match up to your own [windows]. But the sliding glass door allows you to enter that world as well. (Reading Rockets, 2015)

Pop-Up Studio offers a process and platform for students to work multimodally to expand their thinking in new, divergent directions.

Where might Abundance already live in your practice, and where could it develop further? Here are some sample contexts to get you started:

- Diverse books and materials on offer

- Special objects displayed from home or that represent your learners

- Solving problems in multiple ways or from multiple perspectives

- Saying "Yes, let's try that" when learners want to take academic risks

Authenticity

This is important to me, and it's important to others working with this, too.

Authenticity as a principle or criterion for Pop-Up Studio inquiries is about nurturing learner interest as a worldly phenomenon. We know that learning improves when school work is meaningful and enduring. Authentic contexts create a realness for participants that blurs the school-world divide (Paterson, 2010). Learning in genuine ways honours the learner while at the same time invites the tension and messiness of connected and real experiences.

Authenticity is also about being vigilant in helping learners connect their passions to the broader community. In other words, it's about appreciating that the concepts we explore together are relevant and significant to the world at large (Galileo Education Network, 2016). Sharing examples of how others—experts and novices alike—are grappling with similar ideas and compelling pursuits is one way to develop authenticity in learning experiences.

WHY DOES AUTHENTICITY MATTER FOR TODAY'S LEARNERS?

Authenticity is a conduit to worthwhileness. Worthwhileness is all about seeking kinships or bloodlines between the concepts we study and how we compose ourselves as a result (Jardine, 2008). When we deem a task to be worthwhile, we invest ourselves in it. Because we see ourselves reflected and implicated in the task, we invite and accept the messiness and complexity inherent within it. As caring teachers, we want the subjects we teach to matter to our students. Care begins with treating our students as worthy of our attention (Carrington, 2019). Pop-Up Studio offers one way to kindle connection with students by centring their learning.

Authenticity is also a conduit to passion. Today's learners are likely to have more free time on their hands compared to previous generations who, without AI and apps, spent leisure time running errands. Demographers and community-building executives like Natalie Franke are predicting an "unprecedented rise in creativity, education, and self-care with Gen Alpha spending more time exploring their passions, prioritizing mental wellness, and seeking education for the simple joy of learning" (Bologna, 2019). Learners need to develop self-regulation and self-direction to explore their passions purposefully. This happens with the support of responsive mentors who can model and scaffold useful processes.

Where might Authenticity already live in your practice, and where could it develop further? Here are some sample contexts to get you started:

- Role-playing
- Field work
- Mentorship programs
- Choice boards

Awareness

Aha! Yes! It's like...

Awareness sparks new ideas and insights; it is the essence of the aha moment. Aha moments happen when we connect conceptual dots, when we see relationships and patterns between ideas. We'll do a deep dive into conceptual understanding in the Concepts section of the CME Design Framework, but for now, we might think about ahas as two magnets connecting, or a lightbulb going on in the brain. Philosophers such as Slattery et al. (2007) suggest that we cannot force aha moments. But we can design learning environments that support conceptual thinking.

WHY DOES AWARENESS MATTER FOR TODAY'S LEARNERS?

Shifting conditions are part of the human condition. Today's learners will continue to experience a dynamic world, including a perpetually fickle employment landscape (McCrindle, 2020). Aha moments can inspire them to break out of repetitive patterns and help them to grow new schema and dispositions.

Now, more than ever, we need to be flexible and adaptive so we can encourage our learners to be the same way. Helen Timperley, professor of education, University of Auckland, and her colleagues use the term "adaptive expertise" to describe expertise for unstable environments, such as teaching. At the heart, adaptive expertise is about optimising outcomes, being agents of change, and developing self-awareness about one's effectiveness (Australian Institute for Teaching and School Leadership, 2015).

Without opportunities for waking up to new possibilities, the learning experience can be limiting to particular contexts (Paterson, 2010).

> A key finding in the learning and transfer literature is that organizing information into a conceptual framework allows for greater "transfer"; that is, it allows the student to apply what was learned in new situations and to learn related information more quickly...As concepts are reinforced, the student will transfer learning beyond the classroom. (National Research Council, 2000, p. 13)

Much like a composer, we want a student to draw upon and combine ideas as they comprehend, and then respond to the world. As an increasingly global and transient society, we need education models that help young people be flexible, find relevancy, and create meaning anywhere in the world.

Where might awareness already live in your practice, and where could it develop further? Here are some sample contexts to get you started:

- Questioning routines
- Consolidating activities
- Big Idea building
- Data analysis

Anew

I never thought of it in that way before!

Anew fosters deep learning of concepts over time through recursive inquiry. Creating opportunities to return to ideas, to connect and meet ideas again and again as they grow in sophistication, fosters complexity within a study and enhances conceptual thinking (Jardine et al., 2006; Erickson et al., 2017).

But Anew also speaks to imagination and renovation. Anew is at play when we understand something differently than we did before. That is, Anew encourages "the capacity of beginning something anew" (Arendt, 1958, p. 9).

Ron Ritchhart (2015) encourages us to notice the "wow" in each learning experience, to be surprised by what learners say, do, and become. Anew reminds us to nurture the newness in children's interests, experimentation, and theories alongside our teaching, and to uphold these as legitimate entry points to wisdom and artistry. We support students in seeing the connection between Authenticity and Anew when we help learners to see the relevance and significance of their learning now and in the future.

WHY DOES ANEW MATTER FOR TODAY'S LEARNERS?

Although as adults we are responsible to teach children about the world, we don't want to squash the gift childhood can bring: to offer new ways of being and becoming through imagination. Renewing the world begins with imagination.

Imagination kindles play, possibilities, and the promise of "What ifs" and "How abouts." Anew isn't about forced creativity or the pressure of discovering or inventing something "new" for an assignment or grade. Rather, Anew, as the sister of Awareness, emerges when we uncover something new to us personally, to the group of peers we are with, or, just maybe, to the world at large. As stated in the Creative Thinking Facet in the BC Curriculum:

> The idea or product may have value in a variety of ways and contexts— it may be fun, provide a sense of accomplishment, solve a problem, be a form of self-expression, provoke reflection, or provide a new perspective that influences the way people think or act. It can have a positive impact on the individual, classmates, the community, or the world. (Government of British Columbia, 2020)

As an example, today's learners face a collection of sustainability challenges as indicated by the UN Sustainable Development Goals (*sdgs.un.org/goals*). Solutions to such challenges come about through innovative design that requires imagination. Because of this, Anew might be one of the most essential principles for the future of all life on our planet!

Anew also speaks to kindling "the capacity of beginning something anew."

(Arendt, 1958, p. 9)

Where might Anew already live in your practice, and where could it develop further? Here are some sample contexts to get you started:

- Design challenges
- "What if" questions
- Imaginative (fantasy) play
- Composing

The Pop-Up Studio
Design Framework: CME

> " To be truly visionary, we
> have to root our imagination
> in our concrete reality while
> simultaneously imagining
> possibilities beyond that reality. "

bell hooks

The CME Design Framework

Pop-Up Studios are designed by educators and learners using the Concept-Material-Experience (CME) Design Framework. CME, pronounced "see me," serves as an accessible, flexible, and creative planning routine to generate dynamic learning experiences.

Planning for Pop-Up Studio ignites agency by awakening and unleashing our inner instructional artist through the joyful act of creating beautiful and personal learning engagements.

In preparation for our CME deep dive, it may be helpful to imagine the CME Design Framework as three concrete elements coming together as teachers and learners construct, play, and tinker. We "see" this interactive energy in our teacher "moves" and in each learner's "moves"; hence, CME becomes "see me" because we intentionally "see" the person within the learning engagement. When learners and teachers engage the CME design structure as a engaging interplay, we can "see" personal interests, understandings, wonderings, creativity, thinking, and agency surface!

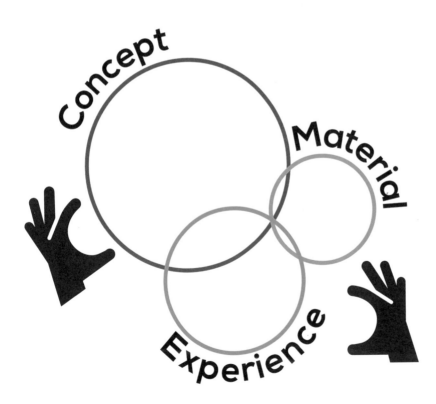

Meet the CME Beads

We will start with Concept. Intentionally designing for conceptual thinking, instead of leaving it to chance, increases the likelihood that learners will come to understand important ideas. The act of developing conceptual understanding lights up our brains with empowering performative schema, a network of enduring, interconnected ideas that we can put to work to help us make sense of new situations, solve problems, create with clarity and purpose, and more (Erickson et al., 2017; Murdoch, 2015)! Consult our Recommended Readings list for more detailed explanations and examples of conceptual understanding and implications for classroom teaching.

Next, we will explore Material. Materials can be gateways into rich experiences, memory-making, wonder, and delight (Pacini-Ketchabaw et al., 2017; Murdoch, 2015; Pelo, 2017). That is why we design for learning with purposeful materials in mind. Materials, if imagined as thinking partners, help to create an aesthetic learning experience that can both ignite and satisfy curiosity (Tishman, 2018). We will offer tips and prompts to help you consider materials as integral thinking partners. While we only touch on theoretical underpinnings in this book, our References and Recommended Readings sections offer a curation of works that can guide your exploration into these ideas more deeply.

Last, we will take up Experience. We are going for dynamic engagements that set the stage for learner agency and self-efficacy. This section is all about designing for tactile learning that offers choice and voice through material play and a driving concept. As with the Concept and Material pages, Experience offers provocations to get us thinking about meaningful conditions for transferrable idea-building. A collection of CME examples, in real-life classroom environments, follows this section. We hope they help you to imagine possibilities for Pop-Up Studios in your context.

Concepts

What are concepts?

CONCEPTS ARE MENTAL CONSTRUCTS THAT FRAME A SET OF OBJECTS OR IDEAS WITH COMMON ATTRIBUTES.

Simply put, concepts are ideas. Relationship, Time, Place, and Self are all examples of concepts. So are Line, Fractions, Character, and Government. Concepts can be broad or narrow. They can be understood in multiple ways at varying depths of sophistication. Unlike topics and facts that are specific to place, time, or situation, concepts are timeless, abstract, and universal, and thus, transferrable across contexts and situations. This makes concepts a perfect anchor, umbrella, or theme for designing learning experiences for today's learners who need cognitive frames that hold up over time and location.

Designing for learning through a concept or "conceptual lens" launches us from fact-finding-land into the meaning-making stratosphere. A conceptual lens, like Interdependence, Symmetry, or Character, expands learning beyond lower-level facts and skills by promoting "synergistic thinking." Synergistic thinking serves to connect concepts to facts and skills through a cognitive retrieval and transfer practice. Let's see how concepts can serve as generative lenses and meaning-making gateways in the examples below.

Concepts in practice

EXAMPLE ONE: COUNTRY STUDY

Imagine that you need to teach a unit on Canada (or any country). We might go about teaching various facts about the country, such as its population, flag, and size. As we are teaching, we hear many of our learners ask, "Why do we need to know this?" or "I'm done. Now what?"

We notice sustained intellectual engagement when we reframe the unit as an investigation to better understand a concept.

Instead, if we explicitly frame our country study as a quest to better understand **citizenship** (or any other related concept), the inquiry becomes deeper, more complex, and subjective rather than a process of collecting facts about one's country alone. Citizenship becomes our conceptual lens.

There is no arguing that facts are integral to a study; however, we do not stop learning once we have acquired subject knowledge. Our personal intellect steps on stage when we intentionally connect facts to their related concepts (Erickson et al., 2017). We have to *make sense* of the facts within our conceptual framework.

In the above example, facts about being Canadian (or another nationality) can become *evidence of* or *examples of* citizenship. Once we understand something about citizenship, we are better equipped to make sense of other contexts where citizenship is at play. Our understanding transfers, or is "put to work," from one context to another. And we don't stop there. Our understanding of citizenship will evolve as we encounter, inquire, and make judgements over time, across cultures, and through situations about what citizenship **means** and **why it matters**.

Try this:

What happens to your thinking when you consider the question, "What does it mean to be an active citizen of a country?"

Imagine this question as a launching point to the country study. For us, this study now sparks inquiries about identity, relationship, responsibility, etc.

EXAMPLE TWO: BIRD STUDY

Imagine a fact-focused unit on animals. We might (re)introduce the children to the animals and present facts about where they live, what they eat, and what they do. But we can then enhance the study using a conceptual lens, such as survival. In order to help the children understand the concept of survival, we might invite them to think about related concepts, such as the animals' needs/wants and the design of their bodies.

For simplicity, imagine the animal is a bird, and we have collected various connected facts about the bird of our choosing. We still engage with facts about birds, but the emphasis becomes understanding the concepts of survival, needs/wants, and design features, and making sense of the relationships between them. For instance, how do needs and wants relate to design features that might determine the bird's survival?

If we intentionally think about and come to better understand the idea of survival through related concepts, birds become one possibility of many inquiries about the survival of living things. By transferring our understanding from birds to another living thing, we are more likely to "see" survival in other related contexts. Patterns surface.

Our understanding of needs/wants, design features, and survival grows, as well as our ability to relate these concepts together.

Try this:

What happens when you connect your knowledge about birds to other living things through questions? For example:

"What needs does this living thing have? What, if any, wants does it have? How does this organism's features help it meet its needs to survive? What happens when it cannot meet its needs?"

What additional concepts could amplify the bird study? What other animals might you choose to study?

Why do concepts matter to today's learners?

As illustrated in the examples above, there are at least three big reasons to spend time explicitly teaching to concepts and designing for conceptual understanding:

1. **CONCEPTS TRANSFER WITH LEARNERS AS THEY MOVE AND GROW.**

   As a world on the move (or in a pandemic lockdown), concepts can be a connective thread as we learn multimodally in varying learning spaces and places (Erickson et al., 2017; Sigler & Saam, 2006; Murdoch, 2015; Paterson, 2010). For example, let's say a child is learning that characters can be human or non-human. This understanding can be found in literature all over the world, so they will find evidence of this concept across multiple contexts over the course of their life.

   It reminds me of what my friend Mikael told me about the Swedish expression, "röd tråd" (literally "red thread"). As I understand it, "röd tråd" is used to describe something that follows a theme. For instance, if a piece of text has a "red thread," it's written with a consistent thought throughout. Just like a "röd tråd," concepts are connective ideas that help learners build transferrable understanding. Who doesn't want learning to feel connected?

2. **CONCEPTS ARE INCLUSIVE.**

   Regardless of age and stage, learners can choose topics of study related to the concept and still learn as a collective. Gone are the days of topic-based research projects where the person studying horses has nothing in common with the youth studying soccer. Instead, learners can connect their topic to a broader concept of Passion or Interest, or any other related concept. And students learn more about the concept because they are studying it from different vantage points!

   To illustrate this point, imagine an inquiry into animal habitats. Some learners may choose land animals, others water animals, some local animals, others exotic animals. As in the first example, all of these topics can support learners in contextualizing their study AND allow for personalization. Choice increases motivation and relevance in learning. Relevant learning is sticky learning.

3. CONCEPTS BUILD EXPERTISE.

Expertise helps us remember, reason, and solve problems. The biggest difference between a novice and an expert is that the expert can identify the big concepts (significant ideas) in their discipline, understand their form and function, describe the patterns they follow, and connect the concepts to solve new problems (National Academies of Sciences, Engineering, and Medicine, 2018).

For example, let's imagine a chef who advocates for sustainable farm-to-table dining. The chef has a deep understanding of the relationship between land, pollinators, community, health, pollution, choice, responsibility, conservation, seasons, flavours, and more, whereas a homecook is learning more basic relationships, like how to pair flavours together with local ingredients. Both are working with similar concepts, but the chef has a more sophisticated understanding and is able to transfer this understanding to novel, complex situations.

When learners connect the concept to the topics or processes they are studying, they engage in that cognitive interplay called "synergistic thinking." This is the kind of thinking we do when the topics or skills converge with concepts as seen in the figure above. Synergistic thinking "requires the mind to process information on two cognitive levels—the factual or simple skill level (lower) and the conceptual level (higher). The conceptual mind uses facts and skills as tools to discern patterns, connections, and deeper, transferrable understandings" (Erickson et al., 2017, p. 11). You might think of synergistic thinking as an elevator moving between floors. The topics are Floor One. Concepts are Floor Two. Thinking is the power engine that connects them.

How can I start designing with concepts?

We start with the end goal in mind. In any concept-based learning framework, the learning goal shifts from acquiring facts and skills to developing conceptual structures in the brain that allow for transferrable understanding. In other words, we move from knowledge and skill proficiency as the end point to knowledge and skill proficiency as the foundation for expertise building. We want to help students "connect the dots" in the subject areas we teach and then transfer their understanding to new and ultimately dissimilar contexts (Perkins & Salomon, 1999).

After years of being a concept-based teacher and advocate, I've seen and experienced the challenges of integrating a concept-based approach without adequate support. But I've also helped hundreds of teachers learn to plan with concepts and transfer in mind. While designing for conceptual understanding and transfer can be intellectually challenging, it is also the most rewarding. It is definitely worth the effort!

Based on the ideas and practices that have helped me, I believe the best way to begin is to be a concept-seeker yourself. Here are five moves to get you started:

1. See concepts in the work and play you are already doing.

2. Understand the relationship between concepts, processes, strategies, skills, and facts as a design structure to build expertise.

3. Differentiate between concepts and topics when planning and teaching.

4. Choose the right concepts within the contexts you teach so you help learners build depth as well as breadth in their study.

5. Support learners in entering the concept and help coach them to deeper levels of understanding.

I'll walk you through a simplified version of these concept-seeker moves in the pages ahead. If you'd like more information, I encourage you to take up any of the Concept-Based Curriculum and Instruction (CBCI) books found in the Recommended Readings list.

Move One: See concepts everywhere!

Let's practice naming concepts in a game I call, "What concepts live here?" Take a look at the photographed work samples below and name concepts that you see at play. The concepts may be from knowledge- or process-based subjects. Think science, math, music, etc. There are no wrong answers, only new possibilities for seeing concepts everywhere!

TAKE IT FURTHER:

Now revisit each photo/work sample and use a variety of disciplinary lenses to draw out subject-specific concepts learners could inquire into. For example, you might ask: What math concepts live here? Then ask: What science concepts live here?

As teachers, trying on a variety of conceptual lenses can help us find synergy between disciplines, helping us to create transdisciplinary or cross-curricular studies. As learners, inquiring into a single event or phenomenon from a variety of perspectives can help us to understand the world in new and deeper ways.

Move Two: Understand the relationship between concepts, processes, strategies, skills, and facts as an expertise-building design structure

Much like animal and plant kingdoms have an inherent structure, school subjects also have a natural organization. Understanding this organization allows us to design learning that is intended to help learners generate and transfer ideas in a way that builds expertise (Erickson et al., 2017). We want our learning structures to mimic those that experts use: "The fact that experts' knowledge is organized around important ideas or concepts suggests that curricula should also be organized in ways that lead to conceptual understanding" (National Research Council, 2000, p. 42).

Two such structures that have become integral to the Pop-Up Studio process are the Structure of Knowledge and the Structure of Process. These structures are used to design CBCI units of study. I've found them to be incredibly useful in appreciating the process of developing expertise.

The Structure of Knowledge and the Structure of Process are read from the bottom up. You might liken this to building a house. Facts, skills, strategies, and processes are the foundation. Generalizations are the roof. Concepts scaffold the two. This analogy is particularly helpful to parents and educators who worry that facts and skills are no longer privileged in an inquiry setting.

While you need CBCI certification to present the structures formally, understanding and explaining the relationship between generalizations, concepts, facts, skills, strategies, and processes is hugely helpful!

Please note: It is worth doing a deep dive into the structures through the CBCI books found in the References and Recommended Readings sections. I will only touch on the structures here and focus on the fact/skill, concept, and generalization levels since those are the pedagogical focus of this book.

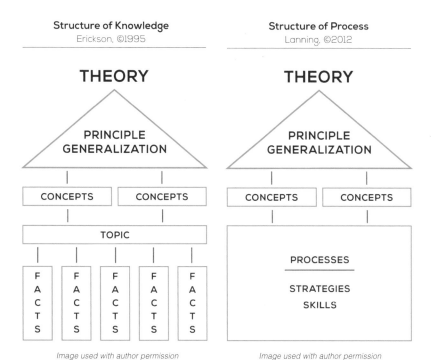

Structure of Knowledge
Erickson, ©1995

Structure of Process
Lanning, ©2012

Image used with author permission   *Image used with author permission*

STRUCTURE OF KNOWLEDGE

Dr. H. Lynn Erickson was the first to describe and model the Structure of Knowledge in 1995, offering educators a clear diagram to illustrate the relationship between:

1. The *topics* and *facts* we teach,

2. The *concepts* that are drawn from those *topics* and *facts*, and

3. The resulting *generalizations* and *principles* when two or more *concepts* are combined to make a sentence of understanding that transfers through time, across cultures, and across situations (Erickson et al., 2017, p. 30).

"We extrapolate concepts and generalizations from the critical factual content to solidly ground our ideas."

(Erickson et al., 2017, p. 32)

Structure of Knowledge
Erickson, ©1995

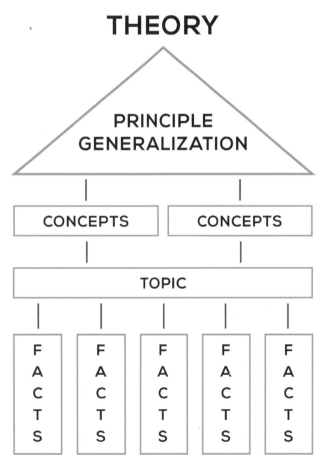

Image used with author permission

FACTS: Facts are "specific examples of people, places, situations, or things. Facts provide support for principles and generalizations" (Erickson et al., 2017, p. 33). We might think of facts as memorizable knowledge. "Paris is the capital city of France" is a fact.

TOPICS: A topic frames a set of facts. Both facts and topics are particular to place, time, situation, or things. They do not transfer. Topics offer context by relating to "people, places, situations, or things" (Erickson et al., 2017, p. 33). While topics are important to creating relevance, focusing instruction on topics alone (e.g., pirates, apples, owls, etc.) can create a fact-finding experience where learner motivation can dwindle. This is especially true when the novelty of the topic wears off, or, worse, if a learner has an aversion to the topic from the start (e.g., my daughter with spiders).

CONCEPTS: Concepts are "mental constructs derived from the topic" (Erickson et al., 2017, p. 33). Depending on the topic, concepts depict various levels of generality, abstractness, and complexity. As such, concepts can be macro (cross-disciplinary) or micro (intradisciplinary). For instance, the concept of "relationship" applies to all disciplines while the concept of "rhythm" develops craft within the arts. Concepts transfer because of their generalizability (Erickson et al., 2017).

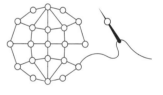

Let's connect the dots in a thread-of-understanding.

GENERALIZATIONS: Generalizations are sentences of understanding; they are also called Big Ideas, Essential Understandings, and Central Ideas. Generalizations capture and describe the way experts "connect the dots" within a subject area. Experts are able to articulate conceptual relationships between two or more concepts with a level of specificity that answers the questions how and why. We want students to "connect the dots" within their study by articulating generalizations. A learner might begin a generalization with the phrase, "I understand that..." Because generalization transfers across time, place, and situation, the beaded globe icon symbolizes a general universal application.

Please note: "Generalizations must be tested against, and supported by, the facts" (Erickson et al., 2017, p. 34). An example of a generalization from Erickson et al. (2017) is: "Writers often create a character's internal and external conflicts to imply a deeper message about life or human nature" (p. 41). You might have noticed the qualifier "often" in this generalization. While qualifiers are at times necessary to ensure that the statement is truthful, frequent use may weaken your curriculum plan. More on the use of qualifiers and writing generalizations can be found in the CBCI books.

STRUCTURE OF PROCESS

The Structure of Process, created by Dr. Lois Lanning in 2012, illustrates the natural structure of process-based subject areas like language arts, fine arts, physical education, modern languages, etc. Because these disciplines are concerned with developing craft, it makes sense that skills, strategies, and processes replace the facts as the foundation in this structure.

"When we reach the level of concepts within this structure, we move from 'doing' to 'understanding' why we do what we do."

(Erickson et al., 2017, p. 36)

Structure of Process
Lanning, ©2012

THEORY

PRINCIPLE
GENERALIZATION

CONCEPTS	CONCEPTS

PROCESSES

STRATEGIES
SKILLS

Image used with author permission

Learning about Lanning's Structure of Process has been one of the key turning points of my career. Before then, I was teaching middle school English Language Arts as bookstudies and a collection of skills, strategies, and processes. If I had understood and applied the Structure of Process, I could have framed our studies as *explicit* opportunities to inquire into concepts. In doing so, I would have supported my learners in developing generalizations that reveal the connections between process-based concepts.

I now appreciate that constructing generalizations in preparation to support learners in doing the same is a difficult but VERY important task. In the end, we want learners to transfer their understanding to new situations. Students who are taught to generalize at the conceptual level are better able to make sense of their world and problem-solve when it counts (National Academies of Sciences, Engineering, and Medicine, 2018). Alternatively, "if students are asked to engage in artificial, decontextualized tasks, they will develop coping strategies that make sense for those situations, but such strategies will simply amount to 'doing school'" (National Academies of Sciences, Engineering, and Medicine, 2018, p. 151).

think dance

SKILLS: Skills are the smaller operations or actions that are embedded in strategies and, when appropriately applied, "allow" the strategies to work. Skills underpin a more complex strategy. Example skills include: identifying important information, cross-checking, and looking for patterns.

STRATEGIES: A strategy may be thought of as a systematic plan learners consciously adapt and monitor to improve their learning performance (Harris & Hodges, 1995). Examples include: self-regulation, itemization, and organization of a list.

PROCESSES: Processes are actions that produce results. A process is continuous and moves through stages during which inputs (materials, information, people's advice, time, etc.) may transform or change the way a process flows. A process defines what is to be done. Examples include: writing process, problem-solving process, scientific process, and research process.

(The definitions above come from Erickson et al., 2017, pp. 39–40.)

Move Three: Differentiate between concepts and topics when planning and teaching

If you're like me, you get really excited about designing fun experiences. If you are new to planning with concepts, you might initially think differentiating between concepts and topics is, at best, just wordsmithing and, at worst, an unnecessary roadblock to the important stuff: what we will actually *do* with our students. But let me challenge you to think of it this way: Teaching that is based on broad concepts, not just facts, and that involves the learner in "doing" rather than in "absorbing," best meets diverse needs (Tomlinson & Kalbfleisch, 1998). In other words, concepts help us design experiences that are not only fun but ones that also meet the wide range of educational and developmental needs among our learners.

Teaching in intentional ways for conceptual understanding helps learners recognize that concepts live *in relation* to the topics and processes we teach, and that concepts build expertise. When learners generate conceptual understanding that transfers across contexts through "mindful abstraction from the context of learning or application and a deliberate search for connections" (Perkins & Salomon, 1999, p. 8), they remember, reason, and solve problems.

Here are two helpful tips to ensure you are teaching concepts instead of topics:

1. Concepts are often captured by one or two words (e.g., war is a concept; the fall of Constantinople is a topic).

2. Concepts meet the following criteria:

   ☐ **Timeless** - The idea is relevant in the past and present, and likely in the future.
   +
   ☐ **Abstract** (to different degrees) - There are multiple ways to think about and understand the idea.
   +
   ☐ **Universal** - The idea is generally relevant across place and situation (Erickson, 1995, as cited in Erickson et al., 2017).
   =
   Transferrable

Unlike topics that are particular to time, place, and situation, concepts are ideas that transfer: **Timeless + Abstract + Universal = Transferrable (TAUT)**. You can distinguish between a topic and a concept by running it through the above criteria.

THE TAUT ACRONYM

Timeless
+
Abstract
+
Universal
=
Transferrable

You can distinguish between a fact and a concept by running it through TAUT.

Here is a fact versus concept example from Nottingham (2015):

Fact: Paris is the capital city of France (locked in place and time)

Concept: Capital city (transfers across place and time)

Your turn:

Circle the concepts and star the topics. The first one is already done for you!

- Pumpkins ★
- Voice
- Systems
- Canada
- Place
- Earth
- Character
- Penguins

Move Four: Choose the right concepts within the contexts you teach to help learners build depth as well as breadth

I recall a game-changing aha for me in my CBCI training: Subject-specific concepts (e.g., fractions or textures) develop disciplinary depth and expertise. Broad concepts (e.g., relationship or system) can be used to make connections between a set of disciplines in an interdisciplinary study. Just like we want to distinguish between concepts and topics, we want to teach concepts with clear intention and purpose. We aim to apply both narrow and broad concepts to our context so our learners gain expertise as well as transferrable understanding.

Your turn:

DETERMINE BROAD VS. (NARROW) SUBJECT-SPECIFIC CONCEPTS

Circle the broad concepts and star the subject-specific concepts. The first one is already done for you!

- (Balance)
- Cause and effect
- Change
- Character
- Civilization
- Community
- Conflict
- Connections
- Culture
- Cycle
- Diversity
- Ecosystem
- Equality
- Form and function
- Identity
- Interdependence
- Language
- Life cycle
- Measurement
- Metaphor
- Number
- Pattern
- Place
- Responsibility
- Rhythm
- Risk
- Shape
- Story
- Symbolism
- Systems
- Transformation

TAKE IT FURTHER:

Based on reader feedback, Pop-Up Studio makers are usually situated in three primary contexts: classrooms in formal academic institutions, non-formal educational institutions (e.g., museums and galleries), and at home. Contexts can be indoors or outdoors, in large, small, and in-between spaces. Consider the next page as your mini-guide to being a concept seeker, and start by drawing out concepts from the contexts in which you find yourself!

Please note: This list of settings is not exhaustive! Please treat the ideas as starting places only.

LET'S SEEK CONCEPTS IN YOUR SETTING!

Zoom into something you are already doing with your learners. What concepts might frame this exploration? Record one concept per hexagon in the chart below.

SETTING	USE TAUT TO IDENTIFY CONCEPTS IN YOUR...	MY (SAMPLE) CONCEPTS ARE...
Formal academic settings	• Mandated curriculum • Mandated content (what you have to teach) • Course syllabus • Learner interest • Teacher interest • Current events	
Non-formal educational settings (e.g., museums, galleries, camps, etc.)	• Current exhibitions or themes • Programming • Visitor requests and interests • Special events • Crafts or hands-on experiences	
At home	• Special events or celebrations • Everyday moments (e.g., chores, errands, routines, etc.) • Crafts, STEAM challenges, etc. • Playtime • Media	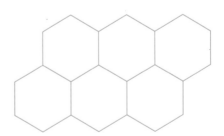

Move Five: Support learners in entering the concept and coach them to deeper levels of understanding

While concepts are found everywhere and come in different "sizes" or complexities, we use our professional judgement to introduce concepts at developmentally appropriate levels with our learners. Here's why: stressful conditions can cause our students to overproduce neurotransmitters that impede learning, yet under challenging students can inhibit the production of other chemicals needed to optimize learning (Tomlinson & Kalbfleisch, 1998). Because finding a good developmental balance with your learners is so important, I'd like to introduce you to the Wild-O-Meter—a pedagogical construct that can help you hit the cognitive sweetspot.

THE WILD-O-METER

During my week visiting Project Zero at the Harvard Graduate School of Education, Howard Gardner, Ron Ritchhart, David Perkins, and Tina Blythe, among others, enriched my thinking about what it means to understand and to teach for understanding through concepts. I recall Dr. Perkins eloquently describing the difference between surface and deep understanding. He employed a metaphor he called a Wild-O-Meter (D. Perkins, personal communication, July 16, 2018).

Dr. Perkins explained that at the surface level, understanding is tame, like a lawn. It is a type of manicured understanding that resembles knowledge-telling. Tasks such as underlining topic sentences or naming three types of forces fall into this category. The lawn, or "tame" understanding, signifies understanding as a possession.

As we travel down the meter and into the wild ravine of the wondrous, the complex, and the marvellous, understanding becomes a performance, something we can use to put to work to make sense of complexities we encounter. Global warming, poverty, and the marvels of the internet are a few examples of concepts that live in the wild ravine. Here, understanding is performative, not just possessive. Once we understand something about these complex concepts, using knowledge we have gained in the process, we can begin to see a pattern or order in the wildness.

EDUCATORS CAN INTENTIONALLY SET THE WILD-O-METER.

Teachers can select content depending on the conceptual understanding they'd like their learners to gain. For example, we can study heroes in very tame ways with narrow examples. "Heroes always defeat villains" might be on the tamer end of understanding heroes. If we study heroes farther down the Wild-O-Meter, we might invite dialogue about sympathetic heroes, their fears and their struggles. Is someone a hero if they have fears? Is someone a hero if they take action, despite their fears, but don't actually save the day? These questions can pull us towards the ravine, inviting us to (re)visit our concept of "hero" and where we might experience heroism in our daily lives.

As humans in the wildness of the 21st century, understanding-as-performance is a critical endeavour and a teaching goal that educators should deeply consider. We believe that children can explore the wild in playful, experiential ways with intentional materials, an appropriate conceptual lens, and careful facilitation.

To illustrate, let's consider what learners might need to discover about the relationships between needs and wants, and between roles and responsibilities, as they move towards understanding the concepts of family, community, and government. The following are sample generalizations:

> **Family:** A family works together to meet the needs and wants of its members by sharing roles and responsibilities within the home.

> **Community:** Community members care for living and nonliving things in the region they are responsible for by contributing their skills, talents, and passions.

> **Government:** Leaders may govern the affairs of a state, organization, or people by creating and overseeing policies to meet the needs and wants of its citizenry.

As we become more familiar with our students and what they need and want to understand, we can design learning experiences at the "right" conceptual depth for that child. We can support learners in moving from tame/simple to more wild/complex understandings or generalizations. Together we can renovate ideas with the chance of creating more inclusive ideals that benefit the broader community.

Wild-O-Meter

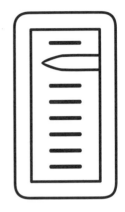

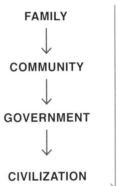

FAMILY
↓
COMMUNITY
↓
GOVERNMENT
↓
CIVILIZATION

DEPTH OF UNDERTANDING →

Your turn:

Let's build onto our hexagonal thinking by articulating the relationships between concepts. In other words, let's practice creating generalizations. Below is a simple scaffolding exercise to build those generalizations. A way more comprehensive approach is included in the CBCI books in the References and Recommended Readings sections.

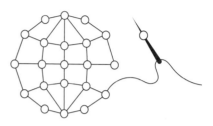

Before we start, it's important to note that while teachers can lend their expertise to novices through scaffolding generalizations, we want to be mindful of the traditions and biases we bring to ideas. Let's hold generalizations somewhat lightly so our learners may renovate them anew. To do this, we can have students use the same scaffolding exercise to articulate generalizations about a vertex (intersection point) in their own hexagonal thinking activity.

BUILDING GENERALIZATIONS (SAMPLE) STEPS:

Consider exercising these steps in a hexagonal thinking routine.

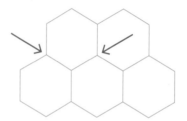

1. Name a topic or example context you plan to introduce to students (e.g., a book about a disagreement with a friend or a process you are teaching like the writing process).

2. Identify two or more concepts you want students to relate (either the Structure of Knowledge or Structure of Process) that are derived from the topic or process. This means the concepts are clearly illustrated in the example context (e.g., cooperation and conflict).

3. Join those concepts together with a present-tense, clear verb. You'll want to avoid proper nouns (so the statement applies across situations) and the verbs "is," "are," "affects," and "influences." These verbs create factual sentences or ambiguous statements.

4. Ensure you also answer how or why. This answer will likely bring additional concepts into your statement, which, in turn, will guide learners towards more sophisticated understandings.

Hint:

Concept: .... Verb: ....
Concept: .... + (How or why?): ....
....

Example:
Cooperation helps to solve conflicts by taking turns and helping one another.

Materials

What kind of materials do we use in Pop-Up Studio?

We curate materials with lots of possibilities for dynamic, tactile interactions. To best understand the tactility of Pop-Up Studio, imagine a materials-rich experience in a restaurant or shop. You're in the shop, senses heightened as you finger or taste the shop's wares. Curiosity, wonder, disgust, beauty, delight, peace... you are awake in a symphony of spatial and tactile meaning-making! You might even feel a sense of urgency to capture it all, to soak it all in because you know this experience is fleeting. After all, you will eventually have to leave. If it was a rich, complete experience, you might even say, "Wow, that was awesome!"

An important difference between a paper-and-pencil engagement and a Pop-Up Studio is the presence and use of 3D materials. The 2D tabletop, desk, ground, or any other physical learning space is literally popped up with 3D materials. Together, these materials can create an aesthetic experience that cultivates curiosity, exploration, new understandings and interests, etc. We find that learners shine when we offer hands-on materials they can touch, move, and transform. This is not to say we devalue or exclude paper or other text-based materials. They are often key materials in a Pop-Up Studio as well. In fact, learners use text-based materials in concert with other 3D materials because we consider each material as a unique thinking partner.

Imagine an old treasure map, a sparkling gem, gooey syrup, crisp paper, a startling fact, a beautiful photo, a tearful letter, a digital microscope—each material has a story, a way of being that can spark memories, invite experimentation, stir up emotion, or kindle creativity. As argued by Pacini-Ketchabaw et al. (2017), "materials do not just feel and act differently from each other, or have different properties, or produce different forms and images. They also provoke different ways of thinking through the subject" (p. 4).

> Learning with affordance-rich materials transforms a 2D activity to a 3D sensory experience.

Materials in practice: An example

WHAT HAPPENS WHEN WE ENGAGE WITH MATERIALS AS CHARACTERS FROM WHICH TO LEARN?

I still recall a game-changing moment for me during a visit to Opal School, a district charter school in Portland, Oregon. I often share the following story to highlight the reciprocity of materials—we shape them and they shape us.

It was midway through Visitation Days at Opal School. I was invited to work with wire and found objects alongside a reflective journal prompt. Our facilitators challenged us to use the materials in our processing. They suggested that playing with materials might help us to connect and transfer our learning from Opal to our current teaching context. I recall feeling stuck and a bit rigid, so I finished my entry with time to spare. I looked at the materials, untouched and beautifully arranged in front of me. A sharp, straight stick of silver wire caught my eye.

Skeptically, I pulled it out of the vase and tugged it down at both ends. It was surprisingly flexible! I continued to manipulate the wire, enjoying the sensation of flexing and bending this seemingly cold and unyielding material. I started to question and imagine: Maybe I was more adaptable than I imagined, like the wire? Maybe I could soften a bit? Maybe I could bend a little more easily? I returned to my reflection with new energy and an action plan. Shaping the wire afforded me the opportunity to see my situation anew.

Pause and consider...

HOW CAN MATERIALS HELP YOU TO TELL A STORY?

HOW DO MATERIALS SUPPORT YOU IN PROBLEM-SOLVING?

HOW MIGHT MATERIALS SPARK YOUR JOY?

Look around your surroundings. Rest your eyes on an object, belonging, or natural treasure. If you are able, touch and feel the item. What are the properties of this material? What connections can you make between those properties and your professional context? How might this material serve as a metaphor for your practice?

Why do materials matter to today's learners?

Materials surround us, and they especially surround our learners. We opened the book with emerging research about Generation Alpha as the most materially endowed generation in history. However, we have choices in how we relate to these items, and so do our learners.

As we saw in my Opal example, or any learning story from Reggio Children (*www.reggiochildren.it/en/*), materials can be powerful tools that can move learning from tame to wild via multimodal pathways. In our experience, playing with manipulative objects (e.g., loose parts) fast tracks deep thinking for students of all ages and stages. This is why Pop-Up Studio encourages a tactile, firsthand aesthetic experience with open-ended materials.

Here are four of many reasons to include objects/materials in your learning experiences:

1. **Materials invite storytelling**, and story catches and retains our attention. We often want to tell people about what we have seen, done, or learned during our interaction with materials. Think of the excitement children have when they master a new skill like drawing, playing a song on the piano, putting together a challenging puzzle, or winning a game. We want to channel the energy into our learning engagements. We want our learners to leave Pop-Up Studio bursting with ideas and insights to share!

Pause and consider...

Think about a time when material-rich experiences got you talking and sharing. Maybe it was reading a powerful book. Riding a thrilling roller coaster. Sipping a cup of really great coffee. Creating art in a gallery. Building a nature-based obstacle course with friends. **What memories pop to mind for you?**

---

2. **Materials provoke curiosity**, and curiosity leads to discovery. A fellow teacher said it clearly: "A touch-and-feel approach to learning generally works for everyone." We agree with Shari Tishman (2018), senior research associate at Harvard Project Zero: "There is so much learning to be done when we slow down and discover for ourselves 'the intricacies of objects, systems, and relationships'" (p. 150). We want to think and learn with materials in a way that feels slow, unified, and complete (Dewey, 1934).

Your turn:

Remember my earlier story about playing with wire? Inspire your own Opal School aha moment with this exercise (inspired by Pelo, 2017):

Grab an everyday object or art material such as paper, glue, tape, or paint. Play with it. Use your hands, elbows, and/or feet. Find out:

WHAT CAN THIS MATERIAL DO?

WHAT ARE ITS PROPERTIES?

WHAT ARE ITS LIMITATIONS?

WHAT IDEAS AND CONNECTIONS POP TO MIND AS YOU PLAY WITH THIS MATERIAL?

3. **Materials invite us to empathize** (to feel *with*). Think of paint, musical instruments, clay, or leaves. Each material speaks its own beautiful language, beckoning us to "sense-make" and communicate with and through them. "We (in Reggio) consider languages as the different ways used by human beings to express themselves; visual language, mathematical language, scientific language, etc." (Vecchi, 2010, p. xviii). Pop-Up Studio, as inspired by the Reggio Emilia approach, is a space for learners of all ages to experience and share the language of each discipline we teach. We do this by encountering and engaging the aesthetic dimension.

   A Reggio Emilia educator and pioneer, Vea Vecchi, offers an illuminative definition of the aesthetic dimension. It is an elusive concept to be sure, but one with powerful pedagogical implications!

"Perhaps first and foremost, [the aesthetic dimension] is a process of empathy relating the Self to things and things to each other... It's an attitude of care and attention for the things we do, a desire for meaning; it is curiosity and wonder; it is the opposite of indifference and carelessness…" (Vecchi, 2010, p. 5).

When I envision the aesthetic dimension, I immediately picture myself in nature. I am surrounded by a myriad of sights, sounds, smells, textures, and tastes. I step into the sensorial enrichment and enlargement of being immersed. It feels like I am stretching into this place, soaking up the vitality with every molecule, being lifted by it, and moving through it. The experience feels cohesive and unified. Like a lit match, my sense of stewardship is kindled, inspiring me to question how best to care for and protect this place.

4. **Materials offer meaningful information**. "Meaningful information is that which is relevant, connected to something familiar, and able to be transferred to new situations or problems" (Zosh et al., 2018, p. 5). Offering a collection of familiar and novel materials that explicitly convey concepts you are studying offers learners opportunities to compare and contrast. As we recall from the Concept section, we need to see patterns and relationships to build expertise. "Comparing multiple examples and drawing analogies between situations and systems are some of the most powerful learning mechanisms available [especially] to young children" (Zosh et al., 2018, p. 5).

Your turn:

Let's imagine that you are teaching about shapes (e.g., triangles). You might put out paper triangles in different shapes and sizes, photos of sailboat sales, a piece of cloth with triangular designs, etc. **Where do you see triangles in the world? What materials show triangles at play in multiple contexts?**

How can I start designing with materials?

It's easier than you think! Let's take it step by step.

1. The easiest place to start might be looking closely at the materials in your immediate surroundings. Pick up the closest object in your reach. Try a slow-looking routine to encounter and explore this object. Project Zero has an amazing toolbox of thinking routines (*www.pz.harvard .edu/thinking-routines*) to inspire slow looking and visual inquiry. Some of my favourite routines are Looking/Listening 10 x 2; See, Think, Wonder; and Parts, Purposes, Complexities. I've used these routines successfully with preschool, elementary, and adult learners.

Your turn:

Now that you are familiar with the material, how might its affordances help you to think about a concept you teach? Affordances, a term coined by ecological psychologist James J. Gibson, are the **interactive possibilities of a particular object or environment or the advantageous properties in a given situation** (*New World Encyclopedia*, 2018). For example, the plasticity of clay can help us think about transformation.

Reveal affordances with these questions:

- How might working with this material provoke inquiry?
- How might this material help inspire connections to people or places in your context?
- What complementary or contrasting materials might kindle empathy and sense-making?

---

2. As you go about your day and week, pay attention to sensory-rich experiences. For example, children naturally evoke and experience the aesthetic dimension when they create play spaces. Children's museums, interactive (hands-on) tinker labs, and maker spaces offer inspiration and examples of touch-and-feel, sensory experiences. And of course, educational giants such as Friedrich Froebel, Maria Montessori, and Loris Malaguzzi left a living legacy of sensorial learning contexts using games, models, specimens, and loose materials. Identifying a sensorial experience is an important start. But attending to how sensory-rich contexts and materials are strategically paired together for pedagogical purposes will take your learning to the next level!

Pause and consider...

HOW MIGHT A COLLECTION OF MATERIALS BE WINDOWS INTO OTHER WORLDS, MIRRORS OF YOUR LEARNER'S EXPERIENCES, AND SLIDING GLASS DOORS TO NEW IDEAS? (READING ROCKETS, 2015).

While there are many examples of Reggio-inspired projects with young learners, I hear teachers ask: What might activating the aesthetic dimension look like for older learners? Here is one example: We were exploring place-based stories in my grade 6/7 class. I encouraged the students to visit a place where they feel their best. Trisha began her inquiry at a nearby beach. She started by looking out into the ocean, feeling the spray on her face, and filling her nostrils with fresh ocean air. She then sat down, notebook in hand, to capture and process her experience in a poem. Later in the week, she revisited the poem, pulling out key words and phrases, and encapsulated it in a handmade container with water to metaphorically represent her embodied experience. Trisha harnessed the aesthetic dimension via materials to develop and showcase multiliteracies.

"[The aesthetic dimension is] an attitude of care and attention for the things we do, a desire for meaning; it is curiosity and wonder; it is the opposite of indifference and carelessness..."

(Vecchi, 2010, p. 5)

3. Now you're ready to begin popping up your learning space. May the next page serve as a spark to step into your artistry. Better yet, invite your students to join you! Ask them which materials they would like to try out, or which might help them explore an idea or help them to address a learning need. Needs may include mandated curricular standards, student interests, conceptual misunderstandings, social dynamics, etc.

Even if you don't work in sites with a cohesive philosophy towards materiality, you can still find ways to pop up a table or small area as a provocation to awaken the aesthetic dimension with your learners. The Preparing Your Space section in the Templates chapter offers practical tips, strategies, and a starter shopping list to get you launched.

ABUNDANCE

What materials
inspire you to
pop up your
learning context?

AUTHENTICITY

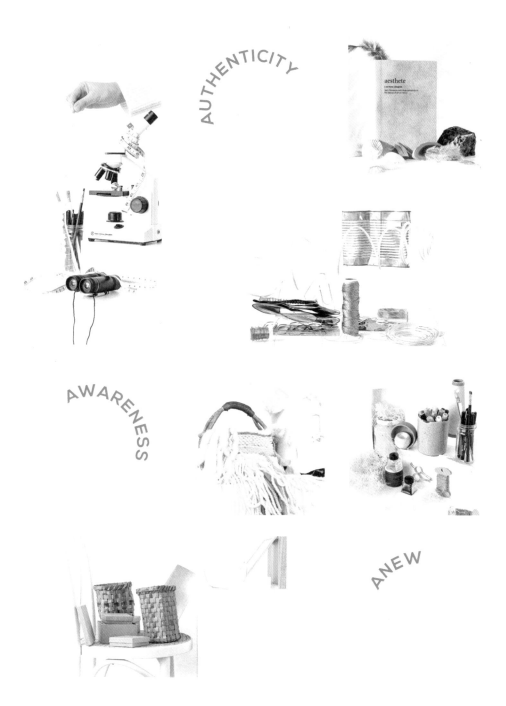

AWARENESS

ANEW

Experiences

What makes an experience a Pop-Up Studio experience?

LET US THINK OF AN EXPERIENCE AS A TOTAL ENCOUNTER— AN OPPORTUNITY TO BECOME FAMILIAR WITH SOMETHING... A SUNRISE, A FIRST DATE, A PLAYFUL PUPPY, A BLANK SHEET OF PAPER—IN A WAY THAT FEELS COMPLETE AND SATISFYING (DEWEY, 1934).

With Pop-Up Studio, we aim to create conditions where learners feel secure, seen, and supported as researchers and creators. We do this through processes and resources such as:

- Careful witnessing, listening, and facilitation,
- Time to slow down and observe closely,
- Access to quality materials and content,
- Opportunities that help students question, and
- Scaffolding to make new and authentic connections to concepts and contexts.

POP-UP STUDIO ELEMENTS COMBINE TO TRANSFORM LEARNING EXPERIENCES FROM 2D TO 3D.

Learners engage in the full experience of developing conceptual understanding by working with the facts, skills, strategies, and processes that come to life for the learner when playing and tinkering with materials.

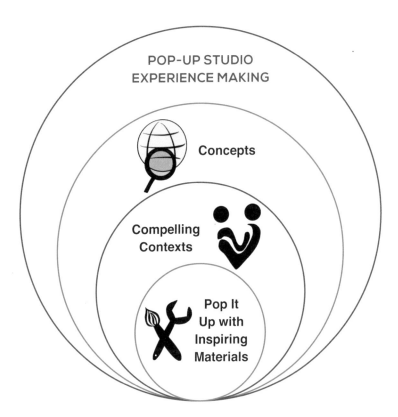

POP-UP STUDIO EXPERIENCE MAKING

Concepts

Compelling Contexts

Pop It Up with Inspiring Materials

This may feel like a lot of pressure. Be gentle with yourself. We have learned that while amazing learning moments seemingly arise spontaneously, they are often a result of an accumulation of experiences (Gardner, 2006). "Each new experience adds to the accumulated meaning of experience for each individual and sets the stage for present and future possibilities" (Slattery et al., 2007, p. 550). Pop-Up Studio experiences aim to wake up and unleash possibilities for learning that endures.

Just like we consider the affordances of the materials we work with, Pop-Up Studio makers evaluate the affordance of an experience. We want to create openings for learners to research and consider concepts deeply with others, in new, dynamic, and developmentally appropriate ways.

Like we read in the previous sections, we design for learning with guiding concepts, intentional materials, and a dynamic context to transform an activity into a deep-thinking, tactile investigation. We know we "hit the mark" when learning feels authentic, generates ahas, and renovates our current thinking (anew) by leading to more abundant ways of knowing and being.

Since we've already done a deep dive into Concepts and Materials, this section will focus on the qualities of Pop-Up Studio Experiences. We'll also take a visit to Janice's classroom-turned-studio. This case study serves as an exemplar of the Pop-Up Studio process in action. Lastly, we'll close the chapter with a collection of CME vignettes and examples to help you visualize CME possibilities in your context. (The Template chapter offers guided support in designing and facilitating your CME plans as a whole.)

Pause and consider...

Read the following quote. Where does imagination live in your context?

"Imagination facilitates creative, critical dispositions toward new content and skills by helping students conjure new connections between ideas and invent new ways to represent and apply information. Clearly, students who are able to find personally relevant meaning in the content and skills they are learning, who are able to envision the instrumental connections between their current work and their later success, and who can dream about a more accomplished life than they currently have are better able to persist and achieve" (Oyserman et al., 2006; Oyserman & Destin, 2010, as cited in Gotlieb et al., 2017, p. 308).

Why use active and engaging learning approaches?

FROM HUMDRUM MECHANICAL TO WHOLEHEARTEDLY PERSONAL THROUGH INTERACTIVE LEARNING.

First and foremost, per the United Nations 1989 Convention on the Rights of the Child, children have a right to educational opportunities where:

- Adults listen and take their thinking seriously (Article 12).

- Talking, drawing, writing and other communication modes are encouraged as a free expression of thinking (Article 13).

- Developing unique personalities, talents and abilities, metacognition, respect, understanding, peace, and stewardship are key objectives (Article 29).

- Rest, relaxation, play, and participation in cultural and creative activities are regularly available (Article 31). (Unicef, n.d.-b)

Second, learning experiences that are framed by concepts and paired with engaging materials stimulate the senses, intellect, and emotions. As such, they are more likely to be transformative, memorable, and valuable for learners. As active-learning advocate Lawrence Lowery (1998) explains:

> The more avenues that students have to receive data through the senses, the more connections their brain will make. The more opportunities they have to explore relationships among data and to use their prior knowledge, the richer and more permanent their constructions of knowledge will be. (p. 26)

Playful experiences with materials are a natural way for young people to learn, but multimodal and sensory-rich learning also helps *adults* hotwire connections and change minds (Garder, 2006).

Third, if you are a parent, an early years teacher, or a play-advocate, you have likely experienced the power of learning through play. Play is our earliest form of inquiry and research. Play is experiential learning in a natural form. However, in my work as a teacher and pedagogical consultant, "play" is often referred to as something that young children do while more "serious" or "academic" learning is appropriate for older children and adults. I'd like to help change that perception.

My research into play, alongside my own experience as a playful teacher, has transformed the way I think about play and its importance in learning at all ages and stages. I'm excited to share the story of how I renovated my understanding of play to the benefit of my students!

PRIORITIZING PLAY: MISTY'S STORY

The biggest impetus for this transformation can be pinpointed to sitting in a Pedagogy of Play workshop at Harvard's Project Zero in 2018 when Mara Krechevsky and Ben Mardell presented their findings based on ongoing research to identify and define playful learning. They listed the numerous benefits of play in the intellectual, social, emotional, and physical domains (Mardell et al., 2016).

While I appreciated the benefits of play, I still struggled with what it could look like in formal learning spaces. Without a clear picture of practice, I questioned how to design for playful learning with my middle school and adult learners.

I got my answer when the researchers shared three key indicators of playful learning: Choice, Wonder, and Delight. They explained that we can intentionally design for playful learning using a tool called **Indicators of Playful Learning**. Here is how the researchers introduced it:

> The [Choice, Wonder, Delight] categories aim to describe the quality of learners' experience as they build understanding, knowledge, and skill. Because playful learning includes both subjective and objective dimensions, the indicators represent psychological states as well as observable behaviors. When all three categories are "in play," represented by the intersection of the circles, playful learning is most likely occurring. (Mardell et al., 2016, p. 6)

HERE ARE THREE REASONS TO PLAY FROM MARDELL ET AL., 2016:

- "By fostering engagement and stimulating sense making, play allows learners to build domain-related skills, content knowledge, and creative thinking" (p. 4).

- "'In playful learning, children are engaged, relaxed, and challenged—states of mind highly conducive to learning' (LEGO Learning Institute, 2013)" (p. 4).

- "...Playful learning engages children in exploring and making sense of the world, while developing self-regulation and agency" (p. 5).

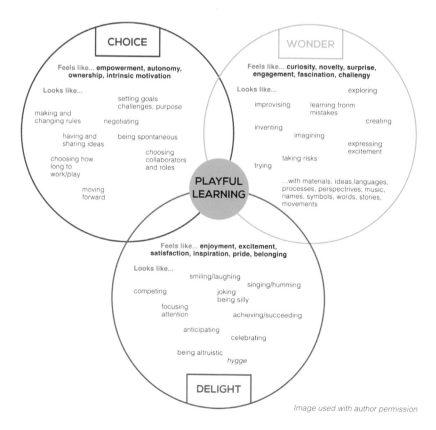

Image used with author permission

The Indicators of Playful Learning clarifies what playful learning looks and feels like. Leveling up the play factor is an opportunity for our pedagogical artistry to shine!

Let's try it!

Your turn:

Take a learning experience that you have designed or facilitated recently.

HOW MIGHT YOU ADD MORE CHOICE? This might look like negotiating or being spontaneous.

WHERE IS THERE OPPORTUNITY FOR WONDER? This might be pretending or playing with materials.

WHERE ARE LEARNERS DELIGHTING IN WHAT THEY'VE LEARNED? This might include celebrating or competing.

The Indicators of Playful Learning helps me open up to a myriad of possibilities for play in all settings, and I hope it does for you, too.

How can I start designing playful learning experiences for conceptual thinking?

DESIGNING FOR PLAYFUL LEARNING + CONCEPTUAL THINKING IS LIKE BEING A TEACHER-DJ.

Designing for playful learning and conceptual thinking is like being a teacher-DJ. Imagine experience-making elements popping up as dials on a planning mixing board. You see a dial for duration, a dial for conceptual complexity (tame/wild), a dial for learner choice, and a dial for the variety of materials. Each of these dials can be calibrated and re-calibrated in response to your learners. These dials (conditions) work together to create a more structured or a more open learning experience.

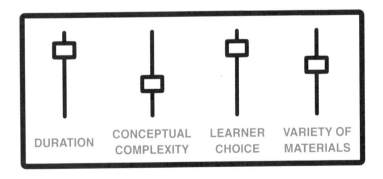

DURATION   CONCEPTUAL COMPLEXITY   LEARNER CHOICE   VARIETY OF MATERIALS

Knowing your learners and yourself is key to setting the dials for success. With practice, ongoing reflection, and feedback, you may increase the level of complexity and choice as your learners (and you) become more comfortable with a flexible and responsive approach.

HERE ARE FOUR WAYS TO GET STARTED:

1. **Identify playful learning experiences that involve choice, wonder, and delight.** I bet they're already in your reach! Think about the choices you offer students throughout the day. Imagine the content you introduce with your own sense of wonder. Recall the delight you see when students overcome challenges or have fun in their learning. Everyday moments can be sources of playful learning when we explicitly name and amplify instances of choice, wonder, and delight.

2. **Build a customized menu of playful experiences.** There are many ways to spark learning. Getting to know your learners and their interests provides a rich foundation from which to discern a compelling experience from a less generative one. Inspiring contexts can be found wherever you are! Ask yourself and your learners the following questions: What do you choose to do in your free time? What activities bring you delight? What places spark wonder and get you curious to learn more? Responses may indicate the kind of experiences you and your learners find compelling. Try brainstorming a personalized menu below! Feel free to use the sample list to get you started.

YOUR PERSONALIZED EXPERIENCE MENU:

Sample Experience Menu

- Storytelling
- Role-play
- Building/construction
- Designing something
- Take-aparts
- Mapping
- Creating an interactive museum display
- Transforming, remixing, mashing-up
- Observing closely
- Sketching
- Giving away something you make + collecting and analyzing responses
- Juxtaposing two materials
- Creating a model
- Testing and experimenting
- Tinkering time
- Projects
- Problem-solving
- Nature walks
- Making (including digital and domestic arts)

3. **Play matchmaker between the contexts in your Personalized Experience Menu and concepts you teach.** Remember, concepts are drawn from critical contexts. For example, number patterns are a foundational math concept. Street addresses in North America generally follow a pattern of odd and even numbers. How might this context spark interest and help your learners understand this math concept? What other math concepts exist in the places you live, work, and play?

What happens when you frame contexts through a conceptual lens or relationship? Much like the hexagonal thinking activity in the Concepts section, notice the synergy when concepts, materials, and experiences converge. What happens when you exchange conceptual lenses— same context, different lens? Revisit your Personalized Experience Menu alongside the questions below to evaluate the likelihood that the experience will support learners in building conceptual understanding connected to their prior knowledge.

Pause and consider...

FOR YOURSELF:

- Where can you find examples of the discipline(s) you teach in your immediate surroundings?
- In what ways do these everyday experiences already serve to inspire conceptual thinking in your practice?

FOR YOUR LEARNERS:

- Where might your learners *already* experience the concept you need to teach?
- What contexts will illuminate this concept in an engaging way for these learners?
- What materials might the learner engage with to find familiarity, curiosity, joy, and transformation as they develop and transfer ideas?

4. **Be prepared to guide the play.** Recent research from organizations like the LEGO Foundation and scholars such as Kathy Hirsh-Pasek indicates that children learn better in playful settings with the teacher as a guide (Skolnick Weisberg et al., 2014; Parker & Thomsen, 2019).
    Unlike more traditional classroom pedagogy...carefully constructed [guided play] situations invite children to take ownership of their learning and to bring a playful attitude to the task. Unlike

free play, guided play channels children's interests and scaffolds their exploration, encouraging a disposition towards seeking out a meaningful learning experience (Skolnick Weisberg et al., 2014, p. 276)

Pop-Up Studio advocates for playful learning experiences with concepts and materials alongside a caring adult as a thinking partner.

Because we want learners to engage in the full experience of developing conceptual understanding, we play and tinker with materials while keeping a conceptual relationship in mind, just like we practised in the Concepts section. We embed concepts in guiding questions to "frame" the experience as a research site for building relationships between learners, teachers, concepts, and materials. Here is a list of guiding question frames to get you launched:

QUESTION FRAMES

Where do you see _____ in the world?

Where does _____ live in (specific context or place)?

How are _____ and _____ connected?

What is the relationship between _____ and _____?

What if we think about _____ in this (specific) context?

How do these materials help you think about _____?

How does the concept of _____ shape our thinking here?

How many different ways can we think about and represent _____?

Questioning helps learners to retrieve prior knowledge, bridge it with new understandings, and kindle meaningful applications.

Questioning helps learners to retrieve prior knowledge, bridge it with new understandings, and kindle meaningful applications. Project Zero has an excellent toolbox of questioning routines called thinking routines. I have used nearly all of them to stimulate thinking and engagement with students. Check them out here: *www.pz.harvard.edu/thinking-routines.*

Pause and consider...

As we move through Janice's case study below and then close the chapter with a collection of CME vignettes, let's ask ourselves: **How can environments serve as playgrounds for the content, concepts, skills, and attitudes we teach?** Young people don't always recognize the real-world application of their learning. Adults can help!

Pop-Up Studio in action: Janice's story

A VISIT TO JANICE'S POP-UP STUDIO PROVIDES AN INSPIRING EXAMPLE OF HOW EDUCATORS CAN HELP STUDENTS TO CONNECT SCHOOL LEARNING TO EVERYDAY CONTEXTS.

In the following case study, Janice works with a fellow teacher and their students to activate connections about the water cycle with previous learning around the concept of cycle. As you read, consider paying attention to:

1. The concepts at play.

2. The questions they ask themselves and their learners to develop conceptual understanding through tactile learning and inquiry.

3. Where choice, wonder, and delight emerge.

4. Any possibilities this story sparks for you!

Now let's see how Janice brings concepts, materials, and playful experiences into her Pop-Up Studio work!

When a teacher for grades 2 and 3 and I sat down together to plan some learning experiences for the water cycle piece of the science curriculum, we considered what the students might already know about water and their familiarity with the concept of cycle. The teacher mentioned the students had learned about a butterfly's life cycle with their teacher last year, so we thought that could be a point of connection.

We brainstormed some indoor and outdoor experiences that the teacher could guide her students through. We began to curate some materials to support our studio work that would nudge students' thinking about the concept of cycle.

- *I thought about loose parts to create models and metaphors with, such as blue and clear glass gems, brown felt for the ground, and sticks and blocks to make trees.*

- *I also wanted to curate items that would represent flow and motion, such as pieces of fabric and arrows. This would be a good opportunity to play with watercolour paints in different forms and using different techniques, so I made a note to pull out my watercolour pencils, palettes, and containers of liquid watercolours.*

- *I remembered a compelling book with photographs of how water is accessed and used around the world and reminded myself to find it. As those ideas came to mind for me, I figured the students might also raise these or similar questions.*

Before our studio time together, the teacher and their students engaged in several science tasks to learn about the water cycle knowledge and language.

- *The students filled little plastic bags halfway with water and taped them to their classroom windows. They were able to observe evaporation, condensation, and precipitation in their bags.*

- *The teacher took the students outside to measure rainfall and evaporation from puddles, and the students investigated some of their own inquiry questions about water.*

- *The teacher asked the students: What other cycles do you know about? How is the water cycle and another cycle the same and also different?*

These preliminary discussions set the stage for the students' studio work.

The teacher asked the students: What other cycles do you know about? How is the water cycle and another cycle the same and different?

When the students arrived in the studio space, I had the word "cycle" written on the whiteboard and asked the students to gather together in our meeting area. I then asked them to share what they had been learning about the water cycle and what other connections they had been making to the concept of cycle. I had curated a buffet of loose parts, a painting studio, and a collection of photographs inspired by the book I had found about water around the world. I introduced the students to the materials they could choose from to further investigate the idea of cycle, asking them to consider what the different materials offered in support of their thinking.

For the next hour, the students pursued an area of interest through materials. This is what developed:

- *A group of students clustered around a table to create representations of a water cycle with loose parts. Some of these representations were flat on the table or ground, and some students began to build up and use the underside of a table as their atmosphere/clouds with the floor as the ocean.*

- *A small group of students gathered to look at and discuss the photographs. I sat down to have a conversation with them about what they were noticing and what new ideas were emerging for them. Two of the students became very interested in droughts, so I went and got my iPad device out of my bag so they could research their questions.*

- *Many of the students began their studio time with watercolour paints and fine liners. I noticed several drawings of the water cycle with word labels for the different stages.*

Next, I added some provocative questions to the whiteboard and asked the students to talk to someone or to think in their head about a question that resonated for them. These were the questions:

- **What cycles do you experience in your life?**
- **What are the similarities and differences between the water cycle and the cycle of a living thing? Might water be considered a living thing?**
- **How does an understanding of cycles help us to make sense of the natural world around us? To understand different peoples around the world?**

About halfway through their time working with materials, I asked the students to pause and take a wander around the room to notice what their classmates were doing. I asked them to make connections and to build on each other's ideas so that they could go back to their own investigation with new purpose and inspiration.

I wanted to nudge the students who seemed stuck on representing the water cycle in a 2D manner, so I asked the whole class to think about connecting their thinking about the concept of cycle in new ways. How might an animal's life cycle and the water cycle intersect? How might a colour, shape, movement, or material show your understanding of the concept of a cycle?

Some of the students returned to their materials and brought in new ideas to what they were doing; others abandoned what they were doing and took up working with a new material. A few students combined watercolours and loose parts, creating a multi-dimensional landscape. I moved around the room, taking photographs and jotting down some insights and comments from students.

As we came together at the end of our studio time, the students shared what they did, what new ideas and connections emerged, and what they were still wondering about. As I shared a photograph of their representation with loose parts, one of the students shared their thinking about their metaphors for cycles as being circles and spirals and how some cycles come to a close while others keep going. Another student commented that a water cycle should be like a spiral, then wondered: what about when there is a drought, when the water stops coming? An animated discussion began around water use and conservation. I was beginning to think about ways to connect our work together around cycles with broader ideas of climate and global issues for our next studio time.

A student wondered, "What about when there is a drought, when the water stops coming?"

Pause and consider...

While successful learning from a Pop-Up Studio endures, the immediacy of the direct interaction with materials will fade unless it is captured through some form of documentation.

As we read in the case study, Janice carefully jotted down notes and took pictures. In what ways did Janice's notes and photographs help the children in her class revisit their learning and create new insights? How did the documentation inform Janice's future plans? Would you consider these practices to be a form of reflection, assessment, or both?

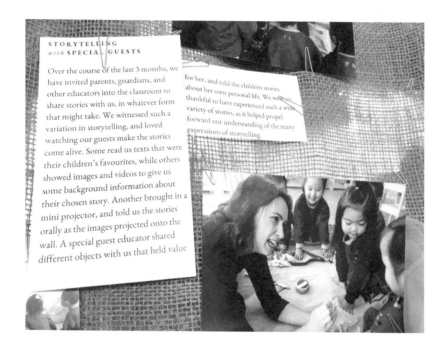

STORYTELLING
with SPECIAL GUESTS

Over the course of the last 3 months, we have invited parents, guardians, and other educators into the classroom to share stories with us, in whatever form that might take. We witnessed such a variation in storytelling, and loved watching our guests make the stories come alive. Some read us texts that were their children's favourites, while others showed images and videos to give us some background information about their chosen story. Another brought in a mini projector, and told us the stories orally as the images projected onto the wall. A special guest educator shared different objects with us that held value

for her, and told the children stories about her own personal life. We were so thankful to have experienced such a wide variety of stories, as it helped propel forward our understanding of the many expressions of storytelling.

CME Vignettes

The following vignettes offer a glimpse into Pop-Up-Studio-making moves with varying starting points but a common material: clay. Each CME story is a single event. Grey circles indicate starting points in each CME graphic. You'll notice a sample generalization in each vignette. This is one of many ways learners may connect the concepts in a statement of understanding. We hope this story collection illuminates differentiated learning and kindles possibilities for your Pop-Up Studio making.

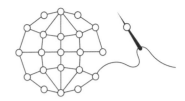

CME MAKER/S: Sam, parent, and Sasha, grade 7 child

CONTEXT: Sam and Sasha are grappling with Sasha's homework: to build a 3D clay model showing how ancient civilizations and modern day civilizations adapt to changing geographic conditions.

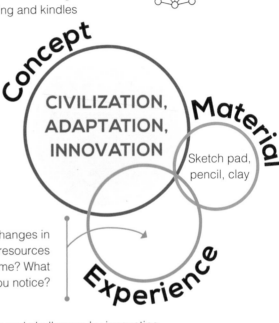

Concept

CIVILIZATION, ADAPTATION, INNOVATION

Material

Sketch pad, pencil, clay

How have humans responded to changes in climate or challenges with natural resources (e.g., floods or famine) throughout time? What patterns or commonalities do you notice?

Experience

GENERALIZATION: Humans adapt to geographic changes and challenges by innovating.

CME MAKER/S: Rashmi, grade 1/2 teacher

CONTEXT: Rashmi is excited to use Anne Pelo's (2017) book, *The Language of Art*, to guide the clay work she'll be doing with her learners. Rashmi wants to create a sensory exploration for children as an entry point into learning about clay as an art medium. She plans to guide the children in associating the playful experience with clay (what it is like and what it can do) with naming the material's properties.

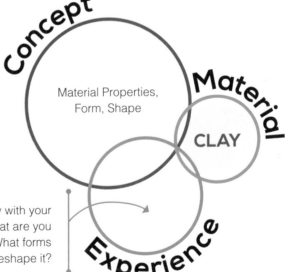

Concept

Material Properties, Form, Shape

Material

CLAY

Feel and experience the clay with your hands, elbows, and feet. What are you noticing? What can the clay do? What forms will it take as you shape it and reshape it?

Experience

GENERALIZATION: Sculptors experiment with the properties of materials when creating form and shape in artwork.

CME MAKER/S: Colby, kindergarten child, and visitors to the classroom

CONTEXT: Colby's teacher introduced the class to the creative projects in *The Stick Book* by Fiona Danks and Jo Schofield (2011). Since then, Colby's sustained engagement with stick transformation, using plasticine and found materials, is so compelling that he wants to share it with classroom visitors at the upcoming interactive show-and-tell. Colby loves to build novel characters and is excited to see what others will make.

How will you transform the stick into a funny or scary creature using only the materials available on this table? What might the materials tell us about your character?

GENERALIZATION: Storytellers (or puppet designers) use creativity to transform materials into characters that entertain an audience.

CME MAKER/S: Amie, math specialist, and Pat, art specialist

CONTEXT: As planning colleagues, Amie and Pat use CME as a collaborative tool to see what possibilities might emerge for interesting project work and conceptual investigations with their grade 5 learners. They start with concepts from their respective disciplines and current units of study. While the starting points for this planning session focus on triangles and design, the teachers soon find related concepts popping up, such as durability, stability, and function.

How might you use clay to design a triangular container? What, if any, benefits emerge by using triangles? What other shapes can be used to make a container? Is there a "best shape" for a container?

GENERALIZATION: Designers evaluate and manipulate a shape's attributes (e.g., triangle) when designing containers.

CME Gallery

The following examples showcase Pop-Up Studio in K–7 classrooms and outdoor settings in British Columbia, Canada. We have identified concepts, materials, and experiences in each sample to help bring the CME framework to life, and we've included generalizations as sample understandings learners may generate as a result of their inquiry.

MAKING JOURNEY STICKS (PROFESSIONAL LEARNING WITH ADULTS)

C: Identity, culture, symbols, milestones

M: Sticks, ribbon, found objects, fresh flowers, fabric

E: What experiences and milestones lead to this moment? How might you use a stick and materials to represent your journey? How might your journey stick help you tell your story?

What do you notice?

GENERALIZATION:
Reflecting on milestones and depicting them symbolically offer opportunities to explore cultural identity.

ADDING VOICE (FORMATIVE ASSESSMENT EXPERIENCE)

C: Typography, voice, and design elements

M: Popsicle sticks, gems, pipe cleaners, and other craft materials

E: How might you use materials and typography to add voice to the important concepts we are studying?

What do you wonder?

GENERALIZATION:
Graphic designers arrange and apply design elements to create typography that can add voice to text.

PLAYING WITH POWER (INTERACTIVE LEARNING SHOWCASE)

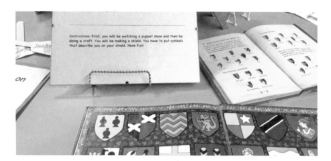

What studio possibilities are popping up?

C: Identity, power, symbols

M: Children-selected materials: books on castles and shields, knight figurines, play castle, instruction page, art-making supplies, shield template

E: A group of seven- and eight-year-old children created this Pop-Up Studio as an interactive way to help classroom visitors understand how power may have been experienced in medieval social hierarchy. They also wanted to highlight the identity-building process of becoming a knight. They invited visitors to "experience" becoming a knight through avatar play with a plastic castle and figures in addition to building personalized crests and shields.

GENERALIZATION:
Leaders assign symbols to property to identify themselves and convey messages of strength and power within a competitive environment.

- -

CONSTRUCTING CURRENCY CONNECTIONS
(LAUNCHING A UNIT OF STUDY)

What's got you thinking?

C: Currency, civilization, exchange

M: "Ancient" coin models, past and presently used coins from around the world, "play" money, inquiry matrix, pencils

E: What role, if any, does currency play in shaping civilizations in ancient times? Today? How might it look in the future?

GENERALIZATION:
Civilizations use currency as a medium of exchange to enable trade.

BUILDING COMMUNITY (FORMATIVE ASSESSMENT EXPERIENCE)

C: Community, needs, wants, responsibility

M: Choice of paints and large paper for collaboration, or loose parts/building materials

E: What does it mean to live in a community of living things? What benefits come from acting responsibly in a community?

What do you notice?

GENERALIZATION:
Communities meet their shared needs and wants when people carry out specific roles responsibly.

DIVERSITY IN ECOSYSTEMS (FORMATIVE ASSESSMENT EXPERIENCE)

C: Ecosystem, diversity, survival

M: Choice of clay, watercolour paints, or various papers

E: What are the relationships in an ecosystem? What does an ecosystem need to thrive?

What do you wonder?

GENERALIZATION:
Ecosystems require diverse producers, consumers, decomposers, dead and inorganic matter, and an external energy source to survive.

PLACE-BASED STORIES (PROFESSIONAL LEARNING WITH ADULTS)

C: Place, connection, story

M: Found materials in situ, such as leaves, twigs, and rocks

E: How are you connected to the natural materials within this place? What stories live here? How might story-making and storytelling make our connection with place explicit? How are connections to place shared and sustained through story?

What studio possibilities are popping up?

GENERALIZATION:
Place-based stories spark and sustain connections to the natural world.

- -

CONNECTING PLACE AND STORIES THROUGH ART (LAUNCHING A UNIT OF STUDY)

C: Circles, cycles, place, story

M: Images from local artists, art materials, loose parts

E: What do you notice? How does the artist use shape and colour to tell a story? How does the artist reveal a connection to place in their art? How might a sense of place inspire your own work of art?

What's got you thinking?

GENERALIZATION:
Artists capture their connections to place (e.g., natural phenomena, life cycles) by telling a story through shape, colour, and repetition.

CAREER EDUCATION (INTERACTIVE LEARNING SHOWCASE)

C: Choices, consequences, gamification

M: Computer, choose-your-own-adventure application

E: How might you create an interactive experience to test out your "if/then" theories? What role does gamification play in enabling people to consider the benefits and drawbacks of their choices?

What do you notice?

GENERALIZATION:
Games offer players opportunities to test out options and theories by creating simulations that can be reflected upon and evaluated before acting out decisions in "real" life.

. . . .

LOOKING CLOSELY WITH DIGITAL MICROSCOPES (FORMATIVE ASSESSMENT EXPERIENCE)

C: Point of view, compassion, understanding

M: Digital microscopes, natural objects

E: How does the digital microscope help you experience different points of view? Why might we need to consider different perspectives of the same event?

What do you wonder?

GENERALIZATION:
Considering multiple points of view sparks compassion and understanding.

BUILDING A SUPPORT BRIDGE (LAUNCHING A UNIT OF STUDY)*

C: Network, resources, empowerment

M: Key words on wooden planks

E: What supports are needed to feel a sense of empowerment? Who offers support to you? How might people cooperate to create networks of empowerment? What happens within communities when someone feels a sense of empowerment and also when they don't?

*Created by Joe McGuinness, Community Engagement Coordinator, Harvest Project

What studio possibilities are popping up?

GENERALIZATION:
Family and community relationships can become a personal support network, offering resources and guidance when problem-solving and decision-making.

ENTREPRENEURS EMPORIUM (INTERACTIVE LEARNING SHOWCASE)

C: Marketplace, supply/demand, pricing

M: Student-made products, pricing, currency, customers

E: How do you determine your price in the marketplace? Will you change your price if the demand decreases or increases? How is price related to supply and demand?

What's got you thinking?

GENERALIZATION:
Supply-and-demand relationships determine a product's price.

The Pop-Up Studio
Coaching Cycle: POWR

> " If we believe, however, that the purpose
> of education is to cultivate dispositions
> for critical thinking, glad collaboration,
> imagining, inventing, questioning, and
> investigating, then...[w]e strive to honour
> educators' capacities to be professional
> marvellers, to be researchers curious
> about and compelled by children's thinking. "

ANN PELO AND MARGIE CARTER

The POWR Coaching Cycle

The POWR Coaching Cycle is a metacognitive process to power up learning designs and conversations. It's all about activating a "marveller's mindset" to hold learning up to the light. The cycle consists of four moves: prepare, observe, wonder, and respond. You'll remember (from the Guiding Principles chapter) that The 4As became an informal coaching framework to facilitate conversations about learning. POWR aims to formally articulate the thinking moves I make during coaching conversations.

Activating POWR feels like a feedback loop or a thinking routine. We use it when we want to put learners and learning front and centre, when we want to cradle and cherish the learning experience. You're probably already familiar with the hard work of assessment. The 4As + POWR can become a tool to do the "heart" work of assessment!

CRITERIA (OR INDICATORS OR PRINCIPLES)
+ INQUIRY
+ CYCLICAL REFLECTION
= JOYFUL ASSESSMENT

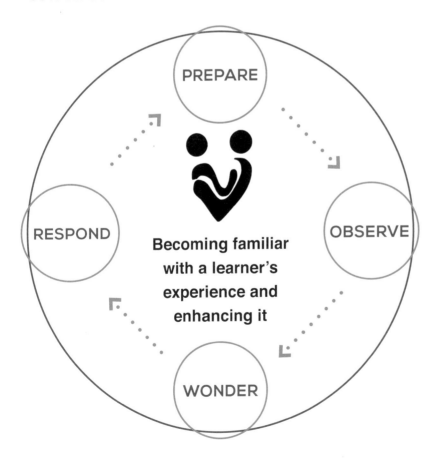

PREPARE

OBSERVE

Becoming familiar with a learner's experience and enhancing it

RESPOND

WONDER

Meet the POWR Beads

You might find that the following moves feel familiar if you already lead learning conferences or conversations with an inquiry approach. If not, the following can help guide your POWR process.

POWR Moves

MOVE ONE: PREPARE
Set the intention.*

MOVE TWO: OBSERVE
Gather evidence.

MOVE THREE: WONDER
Consider optional and optimal responses to nudge thinking.

MOVE FOUR: RESPOND
Engage in real-time.

Choosing your intention, in this case one of The 4As, is like choosing which bead you are going to string next on your necklace. Sometimes we take a long time selecting just the right bead. Other times, choosing feels intuitive or spontaneous. The end goal is to develop a conferring practice, like your personal necklace, that supports how you will enjoy, revisit, and develop learning alongside your learners. Please find a list of questions and prompts to nudge thinking and deepen inquiry on pages 142 to 145.

I hope this chapter illustrates a practical and exciting approach to enhancing your CME designs, nudging thinking with colleagues and students, and seeing the value that your learners bring to the conversation.

Why use POWR as a coaching cycle?

"EVERY DAY, IN A HUNDRED SMALL WAYS, OUR CHILDREN ASK, 'DO YOU HEAR ME? DO YOU SEE ME? DO I MATTER?' THEIR BEHAVIOR OFTEN REFLECTS OUR RESPONSE." – L. R. KNOST

In the context of our primary analogy, The 4As + POWR build a connective thread between you, your learners, ideas, and the surrounding environment. As you scaffold conversations about learning, you and your learners will see not only a thread-of-understanding emerge, you'll see a whole web!

Here are four more reasons why POWR might be helpful in your context:

1. Young people have the right to have caring adults listen to their thinking. If you work directly with youth, you've likely heard the heartwrenching question, "Why don't you see me?" Being ignored or feeling invisible hurts (Williams, 2008). Feeling acknowledged and supported is hugely important for human thriving (Benson, 2011). The POWR Coaching Cycle is one of many processes we might use to realize children's right to be seen and heard.

2. Marvelling with children brings joy. Anne Pelo and Margie Carter, inspired by Loris Malaguzzi (Vecchi, 2010), offer the term "professional marveller" (Pelo & Carter, 2019, p. 59). Being marvellers means that we become researchers of children's learning experiences. When I notice the "wow" in what learners bring, I focus on my students' strengths. When I see learning as a lifelong pursuit, I instantly feel lighter and happier. I'm open to notice joy, activate wonder, find value, and kindle novelty. I am energized! This is true for young people, too. We'll remember from the Pop-Up Studio Philosophy chapter that the way we feel about our work affects the outcome and our well-being. To me, this is what assessment *for* and *as* learning are all about.

3. Observation and conversation provide evidence of learning. Sandra Herbst and Dr. Anne Davies (2015) remind us that assessment is about a *triangulated* approach of **observation**, **conversation**, and **product**. Additionally, Dr. Lorna Earl (2012) claims that assessment for and as learning are still underrepresented in many classrooms. Making metacognitive processes like POWR visible (and critiqueable) can change that.

4. Mindful conversations between adults and children can aid in neural connectivity, healthy socioemotional regulation, joy, and more complex thinking (Zosh et al., 2018). "The teacher's job is to engage in a 'relational creativity' with the child that both revels in the child's creativity and stimulates the teacher's own creativity to find ways to help the child observe, analyze, interpret, and build theories" (Rinaldi et al., 2006, p. 22). As with guided play benefits, mindful teachers can help bring about many benefits for learners, such as creativity, meaning, empathy, knowledge transfer, social interaction, and imagination (Gotlieb et al., 2017).

Pause and consider...

WHERE DOES MINDFULNESS LIVE IN YOUR ASSESSMENT PRACTICE? WHAT OR WHO WAKES UP YOUR INNER CREATOR, IGNITOR, MARVELLER, AND CONNECTOR?

What phrases might help children embrace a creative spirit, observe closely, think flexibly, experiment creatively, and question curiously, all while trying new ways of working? How can we help children sustain the marvelling they naturally do at birth as they travel the grades?

How might POWR enhance your CME plans and learning conversations?

The POWR process is useful for critiquing our CME designs and scaffolding teacher-learner mini-conferences. Regardless of how and when you use POWR, critiquing and coaching calls you to step into your artistry as a professional marveller and learning activist.

HERE ARE TWO WAYS TO GET STARTED:

1. Use POWR to enhance your CME plans. This is an introspective process of seeking evidence of each of The 4As and amplifying your content where needed. You might ask yourself: In what ways, if any, does this learning plan:

   ☐ Tap into the genuine interests of my learners AND develop authentic or "real-world" applications?

   ☐ Offer an abundance of perspectives and ways of knowing to explore concepts and develop new ideas?

   ☐ Provide clear, scaffolded opportunities for developing conceptual understanding and a feeling of being "wide awake"?

   ☐ Kindle new and deeper levels of understanding so we may travel into the conceptual wild?

2. Use POWR to initiate and scaffold conversations with learners using your marveller's mindset to **nudge thinking**. Familiarizing ourselves with a child's thinking and learning requires that we attend to the learner's *experience*. Nel Noddings (2003) reminds us that, "[We] do not need to establish a deep, lasting, time-consuming personal relationship with every student. What [we] must do is to be totally and non-selectively present to the student—to each student. The time interval may be brief but the encounter is total" (p. 180).

Now, let's dive deeper into the POWR cycle, walking through it step by step. Then, I'll discuss the transformations that took place in my own practice as a result of using POWR to activate each of The 4As Guiding Principles. Next, look for the "your turn" box to practice POWR right away. Lastly, the Template section offers coaching prompts and conferring questions to use POWR with learners in your context.

Please note: In the following examples, prompts, and suggestions, we intentionally resist providing a prescribed approach. We do not offer formulaic scripts or detailed blueprints to follow. Instead, we pull back the curtain on some of the ways we work with learners to inspire further dialogue and research. May our journey with POWR inspire you to start your own!

HOW MIGHT YOU ACTIVATE:

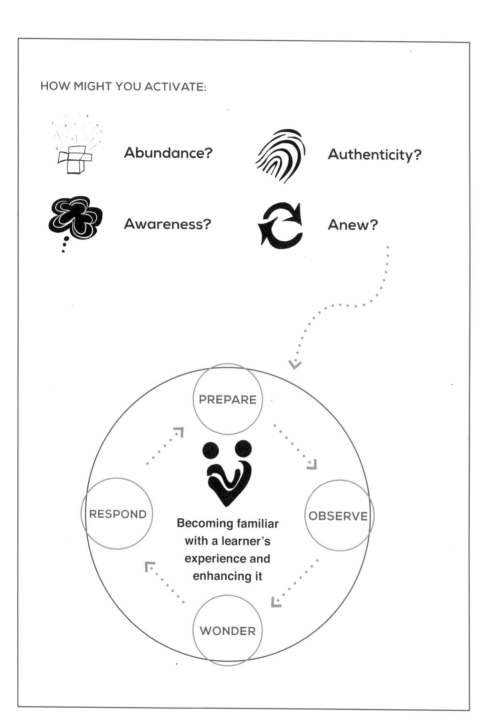

Abundance?

Authenticity?

Awareness?

Anew?

PREPARE

RESPOND

OBSERVE

Becoming familiar
with a learner's
experience and
enhancing it

WONDER

"Observe and
listen to children
when they ask
'why?' They are
not simply asking
for the answer
from you. They
are requesting
the courage to
find a collection of
possible answers."

(Rinaldi, 2004, p. 2)

Prepare

We're going for learning that is authentic and abundant with many pathways and possibilities that will help learners construct conceptual understandings. What A or As might help you scan your learners for generative, playful inquiry?

Choose a Pop-Up Studio guiding principle (one of The 4As) that you want to hold in your mind during your Pop-Up Studio work. Ask yourself: How might I use this lens to see the "wow" in learning or to nudge thinking deeper? You might also hold The 4As in a broad way, using them as thinking partners when you need to invite new ways of learning.

"We each need to take time to decide what it is that we believe education is for and what role assessment should play."

(Earl, 2012, p. 5)

Observe

WHEN WE OBSERVE, WE PAY CLOSE ATTENTION TO WHAT
PROJECT ZERO RESEARCHERS CALL "MOVES."

Moves are intentional actions taken to nudge thinking while promoting
competency and agency. Noticing learner moves helps us to get curious
about learning.

Notice the principle in action and name it with your learners. This might
sound like, "I notice that you are revisiting this photo." Page 139 in the
Template chapter offers a list of Pop-Up Studio learner moves to support
your observations and record keeping.

"Much of education
is about learning
about what
other people
describe—usually
experts—rather
than looking for
oneself."

(Tishman, 2018, p. 65)

Wonder

WHEN WE WONDER, WE ASK OURSELVES CLARIFYING
QUESTIONS SO WE CAN START AND SCAFFOLD OUR MINI-
CONFERENCES WITH LEARNERS WITH A CLEAR PURPOSE.

Example questions may include: In what ways, if any, is this learner inviting
and building on the ideas of others? How is this learner using materials to
activate their inquiry?

Herein lies a conscious opportunity to stay attuned to the learning by
lingering in observation. Give yourself permission to enjoy those extra
moments of reflection. Then, perhaps formulate a response that may nudge
thinking further. If you are using The 4As and POWR as a self-reflection tool
in your planning, this stage invites you to notice biases or assumptions.

"Every encounter
has within it
the power of
enchantment,
if we're willing to
look for it."

(Wagamese, 2016, p. 38)

Respond

WHEN WE RESPOND, WE INITIATE PURPOSEFUL CONVERSATIONS.

We often use a thinking prompt such as, "What's got you curious?" We then listen for the response and follow up with validation that indicates we see the learner. Next, we offer a further question or prompt to deepen inquiry: "What makes you say that?" "What if...?" "Who might care deeply about this?" We might also offer another compelling material to spark new interactions and ideas.

Responding sensitively lets your learners know that you see and value them. A child's attention is precious. It's a fine balance between nudging thinking and derailing a child's confidence or self-direction. Let your sensibilities be your guide as you attune to the way your learners respond to your nudges.

"The judgment of creativity depends on the context...and the stakeholders in that context."

(Beghetto, 2005, p. 255)

The cycle begins anew by attending to how the learner responds to our questions/prompts.

Now let's activate this cycle together as we engage each of The 4As individually in the pages ahead!

Activating Abundance

There are so many ways to think about this!

The lens of Abundance can transform what may seem limited or trivial to us at first glance into a transformative investigation. For instance, we have often heard teachers say, "So now that we're supposed to follow the children's interests, sometimes I can't see the relevancy to the study. What if a child shows an interest in something seemingly trite?" If we find ourselves with these concerns, how can we coach ourselves to be more open-minded or flexible?

One POWR-ful question to ask is:

Where is the learner's interest located in the (broader) world?

HERE IS AN EXAMPLE:

Imagine that a learner is passionate about LEGO. The current unit of study is properties of materials. At first glance, we might not see a connection. How might we bridge the two so that we harness the learner's interest *and* engage them in the prescribed study?

We can invite exploration and connection using the following questions inspired by Agency by Design (*www.agencybydesign.org*):

- **What can LEGO do?**
- **What can't LEGO do?**
- **What are the parts?**
- **What are the purposes of each part?**
- **What different perspectives can we explore LEGO from, such as a toy maker or a plastic engineer?**
- **Why would this individual care about the properties of this material?**

Let's be honest, it is not always easy to see connections between learner interests and the content and concepts we have to teach. Abundance invites us to be possibility-finders and connection-builders. Remember the game "What concepts live here?" If "here" is the child's interest, we may find unexpected and generative connections by thinking abundantly.

I imagine this process as a type of nested experience. I visualize the learner's desired context and see if I can find examples of the mandated concepts at play in that desired context. In the above example, we connected LEGO with properties of materials. While match-making and possibility-finding can be fun once you get going, it is important that the connections are genuine and generative.

> We can honour the learner's interests and address the learning standards by thinking abundantly.

HERE IS ANOTHER EXAMPLE:

When encountering a tree, an artist may notice texture, form, and colour while a scientist may observe identifying features, the health of the tree, and its relationship to its ecosystem.

What happens when we provide learners with the opportunity to try on a different perspective while looking closely at a particular object or system?

With the tree example, we find that acts of noticing from a different role as an artist or as a scientist deepen their respective counterparts. In turn, new ways of being and thinking open up.

Exercising different perspectives applies to material exploration, too. Protecting time to investigate a common material (or topic) through a variety of lenses invites learners to appreciate the complexity of the material. It can also stimulate interest in the topics we are studying.

Your turn:

PREPARE: Choose an object that seems ordinary at first glance, such as a chair, jar, or pen.

OBSERVE: What happens when you observe the object through different disciplinary lenses: scientist, artist, designer, mathematician?

WONDER: What happens when you view this object through a variety of conceptual lenses: perspective, system, play, change, texture?

RESPOND: What role might Abundance play in your educational context?

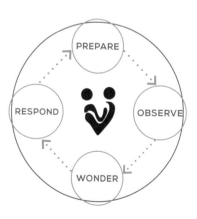

Activating Authenticity

This is important to me, and it's important to others working with this, too.

We know that learning improves when school work is meaningful and enduring. Sharing examples of how others—experts and learners alike—are grappling with similar ideas and compelling pursuits is one way to develop authenticity in learning experiences.

One POWR-ful question to ask is:

Who or what (else) might this matter to?

HERE IS AN EXAMPLE:

When I first taught a unit of study about extreme environments, I had students research various extreme places on Earth, such as Vostok Station, Antarctica, and Death Valley, California. While some children were really excited about this study, some questioned the purpose.

Knowing that experiential learning could further motivate these students, I wondered how I could plan an interactive, whole-body experience.

Clearly a field trip to an extreme environment wasn't possible, so I looked for some kind of simulation idea on the internet. I came across Nuytco, a research company that specializes in undersea technology (*www.nuytco.com/about/*). Their workshop was only a 15-minute bus ride from where I taught!

I phoned Nuytco and begged them to allow me to bring my students to visit their workshop. They generously agreed. My students had the great privilege of seeing submersibles firsthand and speaking face-to-face with engineers who work on them, asking questions about design, survival, and other concepts related to extreme environments.

To see that real people study the ideas we learn about in class went a long way in building relevance in the study.

To see that real people study the ideas we learn about in class went a long way in building relevance in the study.

But realness doesn't always have to come from working shoulder to shoulder with an expert. It can arise through personal experiences that touch us in some way. For example, a child plants a small tree and cares for it as it grows over time. When it appears unhealthy, the child investigates ways to save it. Learning about conservation is a real pursuit for this child as a genuine inquiry.

Authenticity also blooms when we help learners recognize that the concept they are studying in school is significant to a broader population.

For example, a child cares for their tree much like a conservationist takes action to rehabilitate or protect ecosystems. Caring for a tree is not only important to the individual child or conservationist; care, as an idea and practice, is essential for the world at large.

Your turn:

PREPARE: Where do you want to amplify choice, collaboration with experts, or the overall realness of learning for your students?

OBSERVE: Where does authenticity already live in your units of study?

WONDER: How might your learners answer the following questions: *What interests you? What do you care deeply about? Who shares your interest? What methods/approaches, materials, and technologies might they use to develop expertise? What can you learn from working alongside an expert who shares your interest?*

RESPOND: Where might you pop up Authenticity with your learners now?

Activating Awareness

Aha! Yes! It's like...

Awareness sparks new ideas and insights; it is the essence of the aha moment. Awareness and conceptual understanding go hand in hand.

One POWR-ful questions to ask is:

What's the Big Idea?

HERE'S AN EXAMPLE:

Let's imagine studying butterflies. Naming the stages in the butterfly cycle may help the learner construct new and important vocabulary and content knowledge. Transformation, as a conceptual lens in this study, can support the learner in cultivating an awareness of important relationships within life cycles, such as dramatic change and/or metamorphosis. Awareness of transformation as a concept supports further connections to other transformative phenomena in the world, such as metamorphic rocks and the human body.

HERE IS ANOTHER EXAMPLE:

A group of children at my son's preschool expressed an interest in cars. Attending to their interest but inviting an awareness of the concept of force, their teacher offered a variety of materials alongside the cars and asked the following: "I wonder what other things roll? What happens if we try rolling this way or that way with this object, or through this material?" The children were exposed to the idea that other objects, such as cars, balls, rolling pins, etc., can be set in motion by applying force.

"Organizing information into a conceptual framework allows for greater 'transfer'; that is, it allows the student to apply what was learned in new situations and to learn related information more quickly."

(National Research Council, 2000, p. 13)

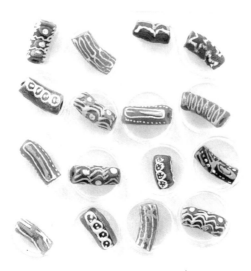

Your turn:

PREPARE: What other "what if" questions might the preschool teacher ask her students to inspire ahas about motion or force?

OBSERVE: Recall an aha moment for you in your own learning. What helped you reach this awareness?

WONDER: What does it look like, sound like, and feel like to arrive at an aha? How might we recognize and nurture this in our learners?

RESPOND: Where do you feel most alive in your learning? What places spark your joy, inspiration, and creativity? Would you describe these places as authentic learning contexts?

Pause and consider...

In what ways have real-life learning contexts inspired aha moments for you?

WHAT CONDITIONS HELPED BRING A SITUATION, RELATIONSHIP, OR IDEA INTO FOCUS? WHAT SUPPORTIVE CONDITIONS WERE PRESENT?

Activating Anew

I never thought of it in that way before!

Anew fosters a powerful combination of imagination and deep learning of concepts over time through recursive inquiry.

One POWR-ful questions to ask is:

How has your thinking changed and what made the difference?

HERE'S AN EXAMPLE:

During an end-of-the-school-year self-reflection, a student makes connections across several experiences that illuminate their deeper understanding of transformation—studying geometric transformations, studying life cycles of living things, and reflecting on how their growth as a learner is, in itself, a transformation. They will meet the concept of transformation again in their academic work but also in their daily life (e.g., in cooking, in the death of a loved one, etc.) Each time, their understanding of transformation can be renewed (Smith, 2003).

HERE'S ANOTHER EXAMPLE:

My daughter and her classmates engaged in a design challenge to create a model of a sustainable city. After researching climate-change topics such as renewable energy sources, and natural disasters such as earthquakes, Eva's team was tasked with proposing and constructing possible solutions out of art materials. Eva and her peers paired their imaginations with their deep understanding of energy needs, fuel sources, and plate tectonics to propose new housing. Rather than large, individual wood houses, citizens would live in connected, bubble-like pods made out of a rubbery, sustainable material. The pods would be powered using solar panels. Should an earthquake hit, the pods would levitate to safety! This project not only taught Eva about scientific concepts, it invited her to think about our own home differently. Solar panels are now on our wish list.

Anew also speaks to kindling, "...the capacity of beginning something anew."

(Arendt, 1958, p. 9)

Your turn:

PREPARE: Think about a concept you are teaching from a learner's perspective. Where might this learner meet the concept again next week, next year, and in five years from now?

OBSERVE: What is the learner's theory on this concept?

WONDER: What suggestions do they have for studying this concept that might offer a new or different perspective?

RESPOND: In what ways, if any, do you hope they will expand their existing understanding of the concept to invite a new or fresh awareness? How do you hope their understanding will develop as they meet this concept again and again?

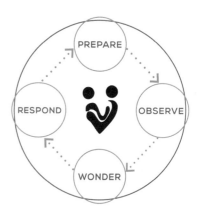

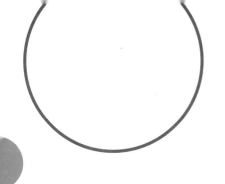
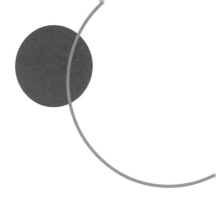

Your Pop-Up Studio in Action: Templates

> " As I teach, I project the condition of
> my soul onto my students, my subject,
> and our way of being together. "

PARKER J. PALMER

**THESE TEMPLATES, ALONG WITH OTHER
RESOURCES, ARE ALSO AVAILABLE ONLINE
FOR YOU TO DOWNLOAD AND PRINT.
WWW.POPUPSTUDIOED.COM/RESOURCES**

THIS CHAPTER IS DEDICATED TO SCAFFOLDING THE POP-UP STUDIO IN *YOUR* CONTEXT.

Photocopy the following pages and grab your favourite writing tool, or download fillable PDFs from *www.popupstudioed/resources*. Want a real-life guide-on-the-side? I can be in your classroom with a click of a button. Head over to *www.popupstudioed/shop* and pick up a book club kit or schedule a personal coaching session with me.

Preparing Your Curriculum

> " There is an awakening involved, I believe, when we learn to notice what is there to be noticed, when we attend to what cries out to be attended to. It has been said that the opposite to aesthetic is anesthetic—being numb, passive, blankly indifferent. Wide-awakeness frees us to see more—the grass, the trees, the city streets, the abandoned ones, the homeless ones, the broken windows, the redesigned museums, what is absent, what is realized. "

MAXINE GREENE

Determining Content, Concepts, and Competencies in Your Context

Our goal is to associate planning for and facilitating of student learning with joy, inspiration, and agency! We step into our artistry when we shift our language from "I deliver lessons to students" to "I make experiences with learners!"

BRING ON THE CREATIVITY AND ENERGY-SPARKING POSSIBILITIES!

Sketch out specific curriculum-related learning intentions in preparation for your Pop-Up Studio. For example, Concept-Based Curriculum and Instruction (CBCI) designers list what they want learners to know, understand, and be able to do by the end of the lesson.

Use the next page as a record-keeping sheet. This record may also serve as your compass or foundational document as you prepare your space and your learners. You may want to refer back to the Concepts section in the CME chapter for specific planning guidance. Remember to consider the Wild-O-Meter so all learners can experience success. You may also want to diversify the critical content so learners see themselves reflected in the context while offering multiple viewpoints.

The Foundations Funsheet: Planning Your Learning Intentions

By the end of the Pop-Up Studio experience,
I want learners to:

KNOW (CRITICAL CONTENT):	UNDERSTAND (CONCEPTUAL RELATIONSHIPS):	DO (KEY SKILLS):
....	....	....
....	....	....
....	....	....
....	....	....
....	....	....
....	....	....
....	....	....
....	....	....
....	....	....
....	....	....

Get ready to pop it up even more!

WILL THIS PLAN:

☐ Tap into the genuine interests of my learners AND develop authentic or "real world" applications?

☐ Offer an abundance of perspectives and ways of knowing to explore concepts and develop new ideas?

☐ Provide clear, scaffolded opportunities for developing conceptual understanding and a feeling of being "wide awake"?

☐ Kindle new and deeper levels of understanding so we may travel into the conceptual wild?

Wild-O-Meter

The Snapshot Planner: Outlining Your Pop-Up Studio

CME MAKER/S:

Name: ....

Studio date: ....

CONTEXT:

- ☐ Launching a unit of study
- ☐ Formative assessment experience
- ☐ Interactive learning showcase
- ☐ Professional development experience
- ☐ Other: ....

....

Concept

Material

Experience

Pause and consider...

1. What conceptual relationships are you inquiring into?

.... + ...

2. What is your understanding goal?

....

....

Hint:

Concept: ....   Verb: ....

Concept: ....   + (How or why?): ....

....

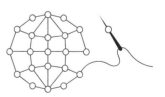

Inspiration starters:

CONCEPT CONNECTORS (VERBS)*

- [ ] Address
- [ ] Bring about
- [ ] Design
- [ ] Expand
- [ ] Fashion
- [ ] Initiate
- [ ] Kindle
- [ ] Model
- [ ] Optimize
- [ ] Predict
- [ ] Reconcile
- [ ] Represent
- [ ] Shape
- [ ] Spark
- [ ] Trace
- [ ] Uncover
- [ ] Widen

Sample verbs from Erickson (2008)

MATERIAL MUSES

- [ ] Beads
- [ ] Buttons
- [ ] Camera
- [ ] Chalk
- [ ] Clay
- [ ] Clipboard
- [ ] Crayons
- [ ] Digital microscope
- [ ] Glass gems
- [ ] Literature
- [ ] Magnifying glass
- [ ] Measuring tape
- [ ] Paint
- [ ] Playdough
- [ ] Photography
- [ ] Recycled materials
- [ ] Wire

EXPERIENCE EXAMPLES

- [ ] Comparing
- [ ] Creating
- [ ] Critiquing
- [ ] Designing
- [ ] Identifying
- [ ] Justifying
- [ ] Listening
- [ ] Mapping
- [ ] Mixing/Matching
- [ ] Modelling
- [ ] Observing
- [ ] Pretending
- [ ] Rendering
- [ ] Smelling
- [ ] Storytelling
- [ ] Tasting
- [ ] Weaving

QUALITY QUESTION STEMS

- [ ] In what ways, if any…
- [ ] What's got you…
- [ ] How might…
- [ ] What if…
- [ ] How about…
- [ ] When does…
- [ ] What connections…
- [ ] Where might…
- [ ] What happens when…
- [ ] What possibilities…
- [ ] What __ live in…
- [ ] What else…
- [ ] When might…
- [ ] Is there another way…
- [ ] Is __ always…
- [ ] Who cares deeply…
- [ ] Who might…
- [ ] Who else…

CHECK FOR LEARNING THAT IS…

- [ ] Abundant
- [ ] Authentic
- [ ] Developing Awareness
- [ ] Bringing A-new understanding

Preparing Your Space

" By creating a transdisciplinary
studio environment, filled with meaningful
and memory-laden experiences, children
are building a reservoir of concepts
and understanding. These reservoirs
of experiences—combined with poetic
languages, materials, inquiry, construction,
representation, community, ingenuity,
trial and error, experimentation,
practice, and observation—develop
the mindset of creativity. "

MARLA MCLEAN

Creating Your Pop-Up Studio Space

As we prepare to pop up our learning space with materials, we consider the environment as a third teacher and how it can support learning through intentional design. There is an artistry in creating beautiful learning invitations that reflect the interests and backgrounds of the learners entering the space. Your learning space may be as small as a plate or as large as a field! Use the pages ahead as inspiration!

INTELLIGENT, OPEN-ENDED MATERIALS AND FLEXIBLE USE OF SPACE PROVIDE OPPORTUNITIES FOR LEARNERS TO THINK ABOUT CONCEPTUAL RELATIONSHIPS IN MULTIPLE WAYS.

With intentional design, a learning environment can empower agency as all learners see themselves welcomed into the space. By providing choice of materials, flexible workspaces, and various conceptual entry points (recall the Wild-O-Meter), learners are empowered to advocate for their own learning and feel that their ideas are valued and honoured.

There has been considerable research and sharing of ideas in this area. We invite you to browse the list of books and articles in our References and Recommended Readings sections.

The Floor Plan: Designing the Studio Space

Indoor Spaces

We have set up Pop-Up Studios in many different contexts. To set a conducive atmosphere for learning, we think about the following physical elements with purpose and intention.

Meeting space:

- ☐ Whole group gathering area
- ☐ Small group collaboration areas
- ☐ Independent work areas

Furniture flexibility:

- ☐ Purposeful use of visual messages
- ☐ White space for eyes to rest
- ☐ Documentation areas

Shelving:

- ☐ Access to materials
- ☐ Items at eye level and below
- ☐ Transparent or natural containers to create invitational displays
- ☐ Uniformed, streamlined, covered, or enclosed containers or cupboards for storing materials

Visual messages:

- ☐ Purposeful use of visual messages
- ☐ White space for eyes to rest
- ☐ Documentation areas

Lighting:

- ☐ Variety of heights
- ☐ Calming when needed; focused for tasks
- ☐ Natural when available

Colour:

- ☐ Colour to highlight a material or an idea
- ☐ A neutral background to allow colours to pop
- ☐ Colour theory and how it supports learning and self-regulation

HOW CAN I SET UP THE FURNITURE AND MATERIALS...

- For comfortable, regulated movement around the room?
- For efficient setup and cleanup?
- For accessibility of materials?
- To encourage opportunities for collaboration?
- To create spaces for close looking, tinkering, quiet reflection, or documentation?
- To nurture aesthetic appreciation?
- For deepening inquiry?

HELP LEARNERS BUILD A CONCEPTUAL THREAD THAT LINKS LEARNING EXPERIENCES TOGETHER.

Learners need to see the conceptual thread that links learning experiences together. Not only do we want Pop-Up Studio to become routine, we also want to nurture a conceptual thread that binds the experiences together. This is in part what separates activity from routine (Ritchhart, 2015). We want learners to revisit their thinking processes as they build a deeper and stronger conceptual understanding.

You might liken this to our beaded necklace analogy: conceptual understanding is the thread and the Pop-Up Studios are the beads. One way of helping learners build the conceptual "thread" is to use a matrix, visual metaphors, portfolios, visual learning approaches, or other concrete forms of documentation where learning is made visible over time.

THREAD-OF-UNDERSTANDING

Outdoor Spaces

Meeting space:

☐ Whole group gathering area

☐ Small group collaboration areas

☐ Independent work areas

Storage:

☐ Secure storage for tools and materials outdoors (e.g., shed)

☐ Transportable storage for tools and materials from indoors (e.g., wagon)

☐ Baskets and tubs to transport and present materials in

Investigation spaces:

☐ Areas for learners to engage with tools and materials

☐ Recording and creating surfaces (e.g., stumps, benches, rocks)

☐ Tarp for ground cover or to provide overhead shelter from the weather

HOW CAN I SET UP OUTDOOR LEARNING SPACES...

• With clear visual boundaries to support self-regulation?

• For accessibility of both provided and found materials?

• To encourage opportunities for collaboration?

• To allow access to tools for quiet reflection or documentation?

• To nurture aesthetic appreciation?

• For deepening inquiry?

The Shopping List: Gathering Your Materials

While we have started a curation list with some of our favourite materials, we want to stress that you don't need to shop or spend a lot of money on materials. Inspiration and resources can be found wherever you are, even with a limited budget.

Tips:

- [ ] Collect materials safely and with permission.

- [ ] The best materials are the ones with lots of affordances, meaning they can be used in many ways to wake up new connections and ideas.

- [ ] Dollar and thrift stores can be fabulous treasure troves.

- [ ] Natural materials can connect us to place and culture but should always be sourced and used ethically.

- [ ] If appropriate, invite your learners to contribute to the materials collection with items from home. Their choices may spark home-to-school connections.

Materials list:

ART MATERIALS

- ☐ Paper: construction, watercolour, cardboard, origami, tissue, crepe, cellophane, wallpaper
- ☐ Paint: watercolour (palettes, liquid, pencils), tempera, acrylic
- ☐ Pencils, pencil crayons
- ☐ Pastels: oil and chalk
- ☐ Markers: permanent black fine liners
- ☐ Charcoal blocks, sticks, and pencils
- ☐ Graphite sticks
- ☐ Clay
- ☐ Plasticine
- ☐ Wire, wire cutting tools, beads, pipe cleaners/ chenille stems
- ☐ Yarn, ribbon, embroidery floss, string
- ☐ Fabric, felt
- ☐ Tape: masking, painters, duct, washi, transparent
- ☐ Pebbles, rocks

FOUND MATERIALS

- ☐ Shells
- ☐ Twigs, sticks, tree rounds and cookies
- ☐ Cones
- ☐ Nuts (allergy check)
- ☐ Leaves, skeleton leaves
- ☐ Seeds (allergy check)
- ☐ Flowers, plants

DOCUMENTATION MATERIALS

- ☐ Clipboard
- ☐ Class lists with spaces for comments
- ☐ Digital camera for still photos and video
- ☐ Acrylic document holder and picture frames for posting quotes and photos
- ☐ Card stock for creating accordion books or tent cards to display quotes or learning stories
- ☐ Empty frames to display work samples

OTHER MATERIALS

- ☐ Blocks
- ☐ Wood planks
- ☐ Corks
- ☐ Popsicle sticks
- ☐ Plastic cups
- ☐ Light table and transparent materials
- ☐ Loose parts: glass gems, small ceramic tiles, corks, buttons, etc.
- ☐ Seasonal items
- ☐ Ramps, balls, wheels
- ☐ Bells
- ☐ LEGO
- ☐ littleBits
- ☐ Magnifying glasses, loupes

- ☐ Math materials: Unifix cubes, Cuisenaire rods, pattern blocks, fraction circles, etc.
- ☐ Digital tools like iPads, microscopes
- ☐ Specialized equipment that those working in the discipline actually use but that is safe for learners you work with (e.g., child-sized hammer)

WHAT COULD I ADD?

- ☐ ....
- ☐ ....
- ☐ ....
- ☐ ....
- ☐ ....
- ☐ ....
- ☐ ....
- ☐ ....
- ☐ ....
- ☐ ....
- ☐ ....
- ☐ ....
- ☐ ....
- ☐ ....
- ☐ ....
- ☐ ....
- ☐ ....
- ☐ ....
- ☐ ....
- ☐ ....
- ☐ ....

The Stylesheet: Styling with Purpose

This spread is dedicated to the role of the teacher or lead learner in popping up the table, picnic blanket, dirt patch, or any other playscape you find yourself in. Like everything else in Pop-Up Studio, there is an art to setting up purposeful provocations. If you have multiple playscapes popping up at once, your Pop-Up Studio may look similar to an interactive art gallery or children's museum, or a workshop with centres and stations. May this page serve as a starting point for careful design so that materials can be generators of human insight (Pacini-Ketchabaw et al., 2017).

> "The experiences you and your [learners] share in the space are what matters, not the formality of the studio space."
>
> (Pelo, 2017, p. 7)

SELECTING TIPS:

☐ Include diverse materials that reflect different cultures and/or ways of thinking/working.

☐ Use juxtaposing items to invite comparing and contrasting or new associations.

☐ Pair picture books, quotations, or other printed materials related to the concepts.

☐ Consider how tools and technologies complement and extend each other (e.g., digital microscope with magnifying glass).

☐ Use felt or woven mats to define workspaces, soften sound, and determine how many people might work safely together. (I like black or neutral so colours pop.)

☐ Encourage reflection and perspective-taking with mirrors as placemats.

☐ Consider including a written or visual prompt if learners benefit from this.

☐ Include documentation media for learners to record their learning, such as digital or print tools (e.g., screencasting apps, cameras, journals, etc.).

STORAGE TIPS:

☐ Use bowls or compartmentalized trays to display loose parts, and make them accessible for hands to reach in and pull out materials.

☐ Store loose materials, tools, and plants in clear containers so learners can see inside.

☐ Large trays can help to unify the objects and ease transportation/cleanup.

☐ Clipboards help keep 2D materials tidy and secure.

STYLING TIPS:

☐ Neutral backdrops, such as wood, canvas cloth, or white tables, can help colours pop.

☐ Consider the flow of traffic around the materials so learners can see and reach them easily.

☐ Balance human-made objects with natural materials.

☐ Use colour to accent intentionally, just like you do in your home.

☐ Play with heights; you might even hang materials above you (with permission).

☐ Pop up paper with a standing frame or acrylic document holder.

SAMPLE PLAYSCAPE:

SAMPLE SKETCH:

DRAFT YOUR DREAM PLAYSCAPE:

WHAT ELEMENTS WILL YOU INCLUDE:

Sensorial Materials (art materials and found materials):

☐ ....
☐ ....
☐ ....

Tools & Technologies:

☐ ....
☐ ....
☐ ....

Storage & Styling:

☐ ....
☐ ....
☐ ....

Documentation Materials:

☐ ....
☐ ....
☐ ....

Preparing Your Learners

"

Learning at any age shouldn't involve becoming tranquilized. Rather, it should involve becoming aware. My role as teacher is to create an environment that nurtures students' capacity to explore the world as it is and to (re)imagine the world otherwise.

"

DR. KAREN MEYER

Leading a Pop-Up Studio

POP-UP STUDIO BEGINS AS A STRUCTURED EXPERIENCE, RICH WITH INTENTIONALITY.

Purpose and intention are key to setting a conducive atmosphere for learning where learners can slow down and embody a sense of flow. We want learners to be clear on what they are learning and why it matters while having the time to raise new questions, explore, and unleash possibilities. Thus, Pop-Up Studio pedagogy requires attending to timing and transitions so learners can go deep within their playful inquiry over time.

Regardless of the number of playscapes or the duration, we want learners to make choices, engage with hands-on materials, and confer with teachers and peers. Building conceptual understanding through accessible material play is a key feature of Pop-Up Studio in action. In short, we want learners to be thoughtful inquirers and possibility finders.

While we have found the phrases, "thoughtful inquirers" and "possibility finders" to be catchy and provocative, learners, especially those who are new to Pop-Up Studio work, need precise and direct coaching regarding the exact moves they need to take while working with materials. For these learners, it is not enough to say, "ask questions" and "persevere." We need to pull back the curtain on what doing so might look, sound, and feel like. This is precisely why we are offering two templates as guide-on-the-side as you facilitate a Pop-Up Studio experience step by step.

Various writers and thinkers detail specific moves that educators can directly teach. We encourage you to take up self-regulation, social thinking, and executive functioning resources to learn more.

HERE'S WHAT YOU'LL FIND IN THE SHAPESHIFTER:

- One student poster outlining possible roles and moves for students
- Three checklists that name teacher moves to consider
- Two sketchnote boxes to jot down quick notes or ideas

HERE'S WHAT YOU'LL FIND IN THE PROMPTS:

- Two options to focus your professional marvelling
- Four sketchnote boxes to record your teaching intentions, keeping them front and centre
- 12+ question prompts to engage learners

ARE YOU READY?

- ☐ I have laid the foundation for my curriculum plan.
- ☐ I have created my environment.
- ☐ My materials are ready.

Now, let's pop it up with your students!

The Shapeshifter: Timing Your Pop-Up Studio

Focusing-In Time

In our experience, students benefit from a springboard to "tune into" ideas (Murdoch, 2015). This is the time to focus the Pop-Up Studio work, to stimulate positive emotions for learning, and to begin thinking about the concept from the start.

DURING FOCUSING-IN TIME, WE AIM TO:

- ☐ Provide fodder for the exploration.
- ☐ Generate data for monitoring student progress.
- ☐ Reserve most of the time for students to play with the ideas inspired by provocations.

The focusing-in stage sets the tone and intentions for the Pop-Up Studio session. It is all about activating the learners' sensitivity and sensibility towards the Pop-Up Studio experience and the critical content being explored.

IN THIS STAGE, WE MIGHT USE:

- ☐ Direct teaching
- ☐ Thinking routines
- ☐ Visuals or visual aids
- ☐ Models
- ☐ Provocative questions

OUR LEARNERS ARE IN FRONT OF US, SO LET'S GET IN THE ZONE TOGETHER:

1. Let's share our learning intention with learners in question form.
2. Next, let's step into our roles as thoughtful inquirers and possibility finders. What do we need to do and be?*

*The time spent modelling, coaching, and reflecting vary with each group. We want to provide access for all learners, and we want them all to see themselves reflected in the learning experience.

> "Preparing students to undertake creative intelligence tasks means scaffolding them in the ability to focus intently on a task at hand and also in consciously, appropriately, and temporarily disengaging from the task to situate its broader purpose in a larger, personally meaningful goal."
>
> (Gotlieb et al., 2017, p. 3).

Print out this page to use as a poster in your Pop-Up Studio!

Pop-Up Studio learners are...

THOUGHTFUL INQUIRERS WHO:

- Ask questions.
- Develop and use conceptual thinking.
- Focus and refocus on the learning experience.
- Notice and wonder.
- Invite and build on the ideas of others.
- Share and collaborate with materials.
- Express their learning (verbally and/or nonverbally).
- Regulate their emotions with support as needed.

POSSIBILITY-FINDERS THAT:

- Use materials to get, build, extend, and re-envision ideas.
- Persevere in their explorations.
- Handle materials responsibly.
- Choose workspaces with intent.
- Begin exploring right away, even if they don't have a crystallized idea of what they want to do.
- Improvise if things don't go according to plan.
- Activate "what if" questions and ideas.
- Look closely, explore complexity, find opportunities (*www.agencybydesign.org*).

MOVE (NOUN)

An intentional action taken to nudge thinking while promoting competency and agency

What possibilities are you thinking about? What moves will help you get into the "zone" for learning in a Pop-Up Studio?

Studio Time

We begin our Pop-Up Studio exploration time with a flyover of the available choices. Choices might include material options or ways of engaging with the experience prompt or questions. We might physically walk the space or lead a demonstration at a common gathering spot. We will model possibilities for working, but we don't always force our ideas onto the students. We want to see the learners' thinking and leave room for possibility-finding. Modelling thoughtful inquiry may include interacting with the materials, thinking about the concept, and/or exploring alone and with others, for instance.

DURING STUDIO TIME, WE AIM TO:

☐ Offer/refine hands-on explorations.

☐ Set cues to transition smoothly.

☐ Protect time to play with new materials before expecting focused inquiry.

☐ Connect with learners (who may be unfocused) before redirecting.

☐ Acknowledge the beauty in what the learners are doing.

Once learners are engaged in the studio exploration, we start and scaffold coaching conversations designed to deepen inquiry and develop conceptual understanding.

MY NOTES:

....

....

....

....

....

....

....

....

Debriefing Time

This is the stage where we gather in a type of congress or community meeting (as witnessed at Opal School during Visitation Days, *www.opalschool.org*). The intention is to provide learners with time to:

- Communicate
- Connect
- Consolidate

WE OFTEN SIT IN A CIRCLE TO DEBRIEF, BUT WE ALSO USE OTHER CONVERSATIONAL STRATEGIES LIKE:

☐ Think-pair-share

☐ Inside/outside circles

☐ Quick writes

☐ Ticket-out-the-door

Next, we offer you the Prompts template, which includes a buffet of questions to attune to the learning experience and launch a generative debriefing session with your students.

Let's weave ideas together!

MY NOTES:

....

....

....

....

....

....

....

....

....

The Prompts: Facilitating Your Pop-Up Studio

Ideas to Guide Your Thinking

Looking for questions, prompts, or springboards to launch or guide POWR conversations with your learners? Want evidence of curricular competencies in action? Pop-Up Studios provide opportunities for learners to develop awareness, self-reflection, and assessment as learning strategies. Use the prompts below to start and scaffold your professional marvelling. They are designed to help you facilitate creative, critical, and conceptual thinking by looking for specific examples and supporting details.

WHERE MIGHT I BEGIN?

1. You might choose to zoom out and observe/consult your group of learners as a whole to see what affordances certain materials and experiences provide. **Option 1: The Panoramic View** is worded for whole-group scanning.

2. You might choose to zoom in and confer with a small group or individual learners using POWR as a conferring tool. **Option 2: The Portrait View** will help you start and scaffold conversations with clarity and care.

3. You might **remix or mash up these options** in your own way!

Option 1: The Panoramic View
For Large Group or Whole Class

☐ What understanding of .... are learners demonstrating and sharing? What might foster and nudge continued development of this concept?

....

....

....

☐ How are learners building on each others' ideas? Are they noticing and sharing with each other? Do they value this facet of creative thinking?

....

....

....

☐ What language are learners playing with and incorporating in their experiences? How does this language reveal their developing understanding of this concept?

....

....

....

☐ Are learners making connections between ideas? If so, what is nurturing those connections? If not, what new opportunities could I present to foster connection-making?

....

....

....

☐ When learners are engaging with a new material, what am I noticing about their process? What might support their use of the material and their understanding of its affordances?

....

....

....

☐ When learners are able to choose their own materials, what am I noticing? Do learners seek out new and different materials, or do they use materials that are familiar to them? What materials might intentionally nudge learners' thinking around an idea?

....

....

....

Option 2: The Portrait View
For Small Group or Individuals

This option helps you spotlight the moves individual learners are making within the Pop-Up Studio and get a more nuanced understanding of the learning experience.

1. PREPARE

During this Pop-Up Studio session, do I want to find evidence of and nudge thinking about:

- ☐ Abundance?
- ☐ Authenticity?
- ☐ Awareness?
- ☐ Anew?

Specifically, I want to attend to:

....

....

....

2. OBSERVE – WHERE ARE LEARNERS BEING...

Thoughtful inquirers who:

- ☐ Ask questions.
- ☐ Develop and use conceptual thinking.
- ☐ Focus and refocus on the learning experience.
- ☐ Notice and wonder.
- ☐ Invite and build on the ideas of others.
- ☐ Share and collaborate with materials.
- ☐ Express their learning (verbally and/or nonverbally).
- ☐ Regulate their emotions with support as needed.

Possibility finders who:

- ☐ Use materials to get, build, extend, and re-envision ideas.
- ☐ Persevere in their explorations.
- ☐ Handle materials responsibly.
- ☐ Choose workspaces with intent.
- ☐ Begin exploring right away, even if they don't have a crystallized idea of what they want to do.
- ☐ Improvise if things don't go according to plan.
- ☐ Activate "what if" questions and ideas.
- ☐ Look closely, explore complexity, and find opportunities (*www.agencybydesign.org*).

Specifically, I am noticing:

....

....

....

3. WONDER

Sample questions to ask are:

☐ What's got you curious?

☐ What do you see? What do you think? What do you wonder?
(*www.pz.harvard.edu/thinking-routines*)

**Note to self: Remember to
help nudge thinking about/by:**

....

....

....

4. RESPOND

Sample questions to ask are:

☐ What makes you say that? (*www.visiblethinkingpz.org*)

☐ What if ....?

☐ What is sparking your interest today?

☐ What do you need to in order to investigate this idea?

☐ How might (this material) help you think about ....?

☐ Who is a good thinking partner for you to talk about ideas with?
How might your materials help you with this sharing/talking?

MY NOTES

....

....

....

....

....

....

....

....

....

....

Teacher Reflection Prompts:

- How do learners respond to different experiences?

- Do some experiences foster social communication and interaction?

- What experiences foster more language use?

- What experiences help learners see ideas in new ways or from different perspectives?

CONSOLIDATION PROMPTS

Think of the following prompts as invitations to reflect, connect, and consolidate. Use them to guide class discussions or feel free to copy and cut them out. The questions then become individual cards for dialogue, sketching, or writing.

What do you know about .... ?

How is your understanding of ....
growing? What evidence could you share to show this
growth? What is helping to grow your understanding
of this concept?

....

....

What materials help you to think?
Why do you think that is?

....

....

What is an experience you had as you worked with
materials that helped you make a connection or have
an aha moment?

....

....

How have different materials or experiences helped
you see things from a different perspective or in new
ways?

....

....

How does being playful with ideas help your learning?

....

....

When you think about experience-making, what starts
the process for you? What is important to you to learn
about?

....

....

What is next for your learning? What are you still
curious about?

....

....

References

Arendt, H. (1958). *The human condition.* Chicago, IL: University of Chicago Press.

Arendt, H. (1968). *Between past and future.* New York, NY: Penguin.

Australian Institute for Teaching and School Leadership. (2015, October 18). *Professional conversations: Adaptive expertise - Helen Timperley* [Video file]. Retrieved from https://www.youtube.com/watch?v=2pE7lbvgTfw

Beghetto, R. (2005). Does assessment kill creativity? *The Educational Forum, 69,* 254-263.

Benson, P. (2011, April 22). *Sparks: How youth thrive* [Video file]. Retrieved from https://youtu.be/TqzUHcW58Us

Bologna, C. (2019, August 11). What's the deal with generation alpha? *Huffington Post.* Retrieved from https://www.huffingtonpost.ca/entry/generation-alpha-after-gen-z_l_5d420ef4e4b0aca341181574

Carrington, J. (2019). *Kids these days: A game plan for (re)connecting with those we teach, lead, & love.* Victoria, BC: FriesenPress.

Cope, W., & Kalantzis, M. (n.d.). *Representation, communication and design* [Transcript of video file]. Retrieved from https://www.coursera.org/lecture/multimodal-literacies/8-1-introduction-representation-communication-and-design-NQgWW

Danks, F., & Schofield, J. (2011). *The stick book: Loads of things you can make or do with a stick.* London, UK: Frances Lincoln Ltd.

Dewey, J. (1934). *Art as experience.* New York, NY: Penguin.

Earl, L. M. (2012). *Assessment as learning: Using classroom assessment to maximize student learning* (2nd ed.). Thousand Oaks, CA: Corwin Press.

Eisner, E. (2002). What can education learn from the arts about the practice of education? *Journal of Curriculum and Supervision, 18*(1), 4-16.

Erickson, H. L. (2008). *Sample verbs for scaffolding levels 2 and 3.* Retrieved from http://pypc2plan.weebly.com/uploads/8/2/0/1/8201588/sample_verbs_for_level_2_3.pdf

Erickson, H. L., Lanning, L. A., & French, R. (2017). *Concept-based curriculum and instruction for the thinking classroom.* (2nd revised ed.). Thousand Oaks, CA: Corwin Press.

Ferguson, R., Phillips, S., Rowley, J., & Friedlander, J. (2015). *The influence of teaching: Beyond standardized test scores: Engagement, mindsets, and agency.* The Achievement Gap Initiative, Harvard University. Retrieved from http://www.agi.harvard.edu/projects/TeachingandAgency.pdf

Galileo Educational Network. (2016). *Rubric for discipline-based and interdisciplinary inquiry studies* [Rubric]. Retrieved from https://galileo.org/rubric.pdf

Gardner, H. (2006). *Changing minds: The art and science of changing our own and other people's minds.* Boston, MA: Harvard Business School Press.

Godin, S. (2020). *The practice: Shipping creative work.* New York, NY: Penguin Random House.

Gotlieb, R., Jahner, E., Immordino-Yang, M. H., & Kaufman, S. B. (2017). How social-emotional imagination facilitates deep learning and creativity in the classroom. In R. A. Beghetto & J. C. Kaufman (Eds.), *Nurturing creativity in the classroom* (2nd ed.). New York, NY: Cambridge.

Government of British Columbia. (2020). *Creative thinking.* Retrieved from https://curriculum.gov.bc.ca/competencies/thinking/creative-thinking

Greene, M. (2007). *Imagination and the healing arts.* Retrieved from https://maxinegreene.org/uploads/library/imagination_ha.pdf

Herbst, S., & Davies, A. (2015, April 27). Triangulation: I understand the "why," now please tell me the "when" [Blog post]. Retrieved from http://sandraherbst.blogspot.com/2015/04/triangulation-i-understand-why-now.html

Hetland, L., Winner, E., Veenema, S., & Sheridan, K. M. (2013). *Studio thinking 2: The real benefits of visual arts education* (2nd ed.). New York, NY: Teachers College Press.

Hofverberg, H. (2019). Entangled threads and crafted meanings – students' learning for sustainability in remake activities. *Environmental Education Research, 26*(9-10), 1281-1293, doi:10.1080/13504622.2019.1664414

hooks, b. (2000). *Feminism is for everybody: Passionate politics.* Cambridge, MA: South End Press.

Jardine, D. W. (2008). On the while of things. *Journal of the American Association for the Advancement of Curriculum Studies, 4,* 1-16.

Jardine, D. W., Friesen, S., & Clifford, P. (2006). *Curriculum in abundance.* Mahwah, NJ: Lawrence Erlbaum Associates.

Le Fevre, D., Timperley, H., & Ell, F. (2016). Curriculum and pedagogy: The future of teacher professional learning and the development of adaptive expertise. In D. Wyse, L. Hayward, & J. Pandya (Eds.), *The SAGE handbook of curriculum, pedagogy and assessment* (pp. 309-324). Thousand Oaks, CA: SAGE Publications.

LEGO Education. (2019, February). *Confidence is key!* [Infographic]. Retrieved from https://education.LEGO.com/v3/assets/blt293eea581807678a/blt38307a01dfe3d171/5fa9426723f3a475feac5c8b/LEGO_confidence_infographic_r2.pdf

Lowery, L. (1998). How new science curriculums reflect brain research. *Educational Leadership, 56*(3), 26-30.

Mardell, B., Wilson, D., Ryan, J., Ertel, K., Krechevsky, M., & Baker, M. (2016). *Towards a pedagogy of play* [Working paper]. Project Zero, Harvard Graduate School of Education. Retrieved from http://www.pz.harvard.edu/resources/towards-a-pedagogy-of-play

McCrindle, M. (2020). Understanding generation alpha [Blog post]. Retrieved from https://mccrindle.com.au/insights/blog/gen-alpha-defined/

McLean, M. (2012, April 22). Happy eARTh day! [Blog post]. Retrieved from https://atelierista.marlamclean.com/happy-earth-day/

Merriam-Webster. (n.d.). Pedagogue [Dictionary definition]. Retrieved February 20, 2021, from https://www.merriam-webster.com/dictionary/pedagogue

Meyer, K. (2008, May-June). *Teaching practices of living inquiry*. Paper presented at the Canadian Social Sciences of Education Conference (CSSE), University of British Columbia, Vancouver, BC.

Murdoch, K. (2015). *The power of inquiry: Teaching and learning with curiosity, creativity, and purpose in the contemporary classroom*. Northcote, Vic.: Seastar Education.

National Academies of Sciences, Engineering, and Medicine. (2018). *How people learn II: Learners, contexts, and cultures*. Washington, DC: The National Academies Press.

National Research Council. (2000). *How people learn: Brain, mind, experience, and school: Expanded edition*. Washington, DC: The National Academies Press.

New London Group. (1996). A pedagogy of multiliteracies: Designing social futures. *Harvard Educational Review, 66*(1), 60-92.

New World Encyclopedia. (2018, March 11). J. J. Gibson. Retrieved from https://www.newworldencyclopedia.org/p/index.php?title=J._J._Gibson&oldid=1009677

Noddings, N. (2003). *Caring: A feminine approach to ethics and moral education* (2nd ed.). Berkeley and Los Angeles, CA: University of California Press.

Nottingham, J. (2015, November 23). *James Nottingham's learning challenge (learning pit) animation* [Video file]. Retrieved from https://www.youtube.com/watch?v=3IMUAOhuO78

Odegard, N. (2012). When matter comes to matter – working pedagogically with junk materials. *Education Inquiry, 3*(3), 387-400. doi:10.3402/edui.v3i3.22042

Organization for Economic Co-operation and Development (OECD). (2009). Teaching practices, teachers' beliefs and attitudes. In *Creating effective teaching and learning environments: First results from TALIS* (pp. 87-135) Retrieved from https://www.oecd.org/berlin/43541655.pdf

OECD/Asia Society. (2018). *Teaching for global competence in a rapidly changing world*. New York, NY: OECD Publishing, Paris/Asia Society. Retrieved from https://doi.org/10.1787/9789264289024-en

Pacini-Ketchabaw, V., Kind, S., & Kocher, L. (2017). *Encounters with materials in early childhood education*. New York, NY: Routledge.

Palmer, P. J. (2007). *The courage to teach: Exploring the inner landscape of a teacher's life*. San Francisco, CA: Jossey-Bass.

Parker, R., & Thomsen, B. S. (2019, March). *Learning through play at school: A study of playful integrated pedagogies that foster children's holistic skills development in the primary school classroom* [White paper]. The LEGO Foundation. Retrieved from https://www.LEGOfoundation.com/media/1687/learning-through-play-school.pdf

Paterson, M. A. (2010). *Living inquiry as pedagogy* (Master's thesis). University of British Columbia, Vancouver, BC. Retrieved from https://open.library.ubc.ca/cIRcle/collections/ubctheses/24/items/1.0069060

Pelo, A. (2017). *The language of art: Inquiry-based studio practices in early childhood settings* (2nd ed.). St. Paul, MN: Red Leaf Press.

Pelo, A., & Carter, M. (2019). *From teaching to thinking: A pedagogy for reimagining our work*. Lincoln, NE: Exchange Press.

Perkins, D., & Salomon, G. (1999). Transfer of learning. *International Encyclopedia of Learning* (2nd ed.). Oxford, England: Pergamon Press.

Pinsker, J. (2020, February 21). Oh no, they've come up with another generational label. *The Atlantic*. Retrieved from https://www.theatlantic.com/family/archive/2020/02/generation-after-gen-z-named-alpha/606862

Reading Rockets. (2015, January 30). *Mirrors, windows and sliding doors* [Video file]. Retrieved from https://www.youtube.com/watch?v=_AAu58SNSyc

Rinaldi, C. (2004). The relationship between documentation and assessment. *Innovations in early education: The international Reggio exchange, 11*(1), 1-4.

Rinaldi, C., & Lally, J. R. (Ed.), & Mangione, P. L. (Ed.), & Greenwald, D. (Ed.). (2006). Creativity, shared meaning, and relationships. *Concepts for care: 20 essays on infant/toddler development and learning*. San Francisco, CA: WestEd.

Ritchhart, R. (2015). *Creating cultures of thinking: The 8 forces we must master to truly transform our schools*. San Francisco, CA: Jossey-Bass.

Rüsselbæk Hansen, D. R., & Phelan, A. M. (2019). Taste for democracy: A critique of the mechanical paradigm in education. *Research in Education, 103*(1), 34-48.

Schmid, R. (2018). Pockets of excellence: Teacher beliefs and behaviors that lead to high student achievement at low achieving schools. *SAGE Open, 8*(3), 1-10. doi:10.1177/2158244018797238

Sigler, E. A., & Saam, J. (2006). Teacher candidates' conceptual understanding of conceptual learning: From theory to practice. *Journal of Scholarship of Teaching and Learning, 6*(1), 118-126.

Skolnick Weisberg, D., Hirsh-Pasek, K., Michnick Golinkoff, R., & McCandliss, B. D. (2014). Mise en place: Setting the stage for thought and action. *Trends in Cognitive Sciences, 18*(6), 276-278. doi:http://dx.doi.org/10.1016/j.tics.2014.02.012

Slattery, P., Kransy, K., & O'Malley, M. (2007). Hermeneutics, aesthetics, and the quest for answerability: A dialogic possibility for reconceptualizing the interpretive process in curriculum studies. *Journal of Curriculum Studies, 39*(5), 537-558.

Smith, D. G. (2003). *Teaching in global times*. Edmonton, AB: Pedagon Press.

Spencer, J. (2017, September 29). We need to trust teachers to innovate [Blog post]. Retrieved from http://www.spencerauthor.com/teachers-innovate/

Tishman, S. (2018). *Slow looking: The art and practice of learning through observation*. New York, NY: Routledge.

Tomlinson, C. A., & Kalbfleisch, M. L. (1998). Teach me, teach my brain: A call for differentiated classrooms. *Educational Leadership, 56*(3), 52-55.

UNESCO Institute for Statistics (2016). *The world needs almost 69 million new teachers to reach the 2030 education goals* [Fact Sheet]. Retrieved from https://unesdoc.unesco.org/ark:/48223/pf0000246124

Unicef. (n.d.-a). *The convention on the rights of the child: The child-friendly version*. Retrieved from https://www.unicef.org/sop/convention-rights-child-child-friendly-version

Unicef. (n.d.-b). *Reimagine education*. Retrieved from https://www.unicef.org/reimagine/education

Vecchi, V. (2010). *Art and creativity in Reggio Emilia: Exploring the role and potential of ateliers in early childhood education* (1st ed.). New York, NY: Routledge.

Wagamese, R. (2016). *Embers: One Ojibway's meditations*. Madeira Park, BC: Douglas and McIntyre.

Wiliam, D. (2016, July 15). *Dylan Wiliam: Formative assessment* [Video file]. Retrieved from https://youtu.be/sYdVe5O7KBE

Williams, K. D. (2008). Teaching and learning guide for: 'Ostracism: The kiss of social death.' *Social and Personality Psychology Compass, 2*(3), 1539-1546. doi:10.1111/j.1751-9004.2008.00101.x

Zosh, J. M., Hirsh-Pasek, K., Hopkins, E. J., Jensen, H., Liu, C., Neale, D., Solis, S. L., & Whitebread, D. (2018). Accessing the inaccessible: Redefining play as a spectrum. *Frontiers in Psychology, 9*(1124), 1-12. doi:10.3389/fpsyg.2018.01124

Recommended Readings

Aoki, T. (2005). The child-centered curriculum: Where is the social in pedocentricism? In W. Pinar & R. Irwin (Eds.), *Curriculum in a new key: The collected works of Ted T. Aoki* (pp. 279-289). Mahwah, NJ: Lawrence Erlbaum.

Battiste, M. (2017). *Decolonizing education: Nourishing the learning spirit.* Saskatoon, SK: Purich Publishing Limited.

Costa, A., & Kallick, B. (2004). *Assessment strategies for self-directing learning.* Thousand Oaks, CA: Corwin Press.

Daly, L., & Beloglovsky, M. (2014-2020). *Loose parts* [set of 4 books]. St. Paul, MN: Redleaf Press.

Daly, L., & Beloglovsky, M. (2015). *Early learning theories made visible.* St. Paul, MN: Redleaf Press.

Garcia Winner, M., Hendrix, R. E., Zweber Palmer, K., & Tarshis, N. (2016). *We thinkers! Vol. 2: Social problem solvers deluxe package.* Santa Clara, CA: Social Thinking.

Kimmerer, R. W. (2013). *Braiding sweetgrass: Indigenous wisdom, scientific knowledge and the teachings of plants.* Minneapolis, MN: Milkweed Editions.

Krishnamurti, J. (1953). *Education and the significance of life.* New York, NY: HarperCollins.

Lanning, L. A. (2013). *Designing a concept-based curriculum for English language arts: Meeting the common core with intellectual integrity, K-12.* Thousand Oaks, CA: Corwin Press.

Lanning, L. A., & Brown, T. (2019). *Concept-based literacy lessons: Designing learning to ignite understanding and transfer.* Thousand Oaks, CA: Corwin Press.

MacKay, S. H. (2021). *Story workshop: New possibilities for young writers.* Portsmouth, NH: Heinemann.

Mitchell, K. L. (2018). *Experience inquiry: 5 powerful strategies, 50 practical experiences.* Thousand Oaks, CA: Corwin Press.

Opal School Publications listed here: https://opalschool.org/publications/

Ostroff, W. (2016). *Cultivating curiosity in K-12 classrooms: How to promote and sustain deep learning.* Alexandria, VA: ASCD.

OWP/P Architects, VS Furniture, & Bruce Mau Design. (2010). *The third teacher: 79 ways you can use design to transform teaching & learning.* New York, NY: Abrams Books.

Pacini-Ketchabaw, V., Nxumalo, F., Kocher, L., Elliot, E., & Sanchez, A. (2015). *Journeys: Reconceptualizing early childhood practices through pedagogical narration.* North York, ON: University of Toronto Press.

Perkins, D. N., & Salomon, G. (1988). Teaching for transfer. *Educational Leadership, 46*(1) 22-32. Retrieved from http://www.ascd.org/ASCD/pdf/journals/ed_lead/el_198809_perkins.pdf

Ritchhart, R., Church, M., & Morrison, K. (2011). *Making thinking visible: How to promote engagement, understanding, and independence for all learners.* San Francisco, CA: Jossey-Bass.

Salesses, M. (2021). *Craft in the real world: Rethinking fiction writing and workshopping.* Berkeley, CA: Catapult.

Stern, J., Lauriault, N., & Ferraro, K. (2017). *Tools for teaching conceptual understanding, elementary: Harnessing the power of natural curiosity for learning that transfers.* Thousand Oaks, CA: Corwin Press.

Stockman, A. (2021). *Creating inclusive writing environments in the K-12 classroom: Reluctance, resistance, and strategies that make a difference.* New York, NY: Routledge.

Timperley, H. (2011). *Realizing the power of professional learning.* Berkshire, UK: Open University Press.

van Manen, M. (2002). *The tone of teaching: The language of pedagogy.* London, ON: Althouse Press.

Wathall, J. (2016). *Concept-based mathematics: Teaching for deep understanding in secondary classrooms.* Thousand Oaks, CA: Corwin Press.

We're better together.

Please share your stories.

—Misty

FOR MORE RESOURCES TO COMPLEMENT THIS BOOK, PLEASE VISIT WWW.POPUPSTUDIOED.COM.